Praise for *Sippy Cups Are Not for Chardonnay*

"The kind of snarky straight talk you'd get from your best girl-friend."

—UrbanBaby.com

"Stefanie Wilder-Taylor offers a funny look at new motherhood . . . If you want to get inside a new mom's neurosis . . . this book is for you."

—*Chicago Tribune*

"Her sharp wit takes center stage . . . This little volume is perfect for spreading some joy on Mother's Day."

—*BookPage*

"Her common-sense advice is a much-needed reality check to a new mom, and a funny, relaxed, assuring breath of fresh air to a seasoned mom. Oh yes, mamas, a great read."

—TheDailyStroll.com

"Her familiarity with the comic aspects of life serves her well, but the book is also jam-packed with information. Every new mom has to learn these things, so why not enjoy some laughs along the way?"

—*Hartford Courant*

"You can't help but love her. The world would be a better place if she were the head Mommy."

—*Mississippi Press*

Also by Stefanie Wilder-Taylor

Sippy Cups Are Not for Chardonnay

Naptime Is the New Happy Hour

and OTHER WAYS TODDLERS TURN YOUR LIFE UPSIDE DOWN

by Stefanie Wilder-Taylor

SSE

SIMON SPOTLIGHT ENTERTAINMENT

New York   London   Toronto   Sydney

NOTE TO READER:
Names and identifying characteristics of some of the individuals portrayed in this book have been changed.

S|S|E
SIMON SPOTLIGHT ENTERTAINMENT
An imprint of Simon & Schuster
1230 Avenue of the Americas, New York, New York 10020
Copyright © 2008 by Jitters Productions, Inc.

SIMON SPOTLIGHT ENTERTAINMENT and colophon are trademarks of Simon & Schuster, Inc.
For information about special discounts for bulk purchases, please contact Simon & Schuster Special Sales at 1-800-456-6798 or business@simonandschuster.com
Manufactured in the United States of America
First Simon Spotlight Entertainment trade paperback edition March 2008
10 9 8 7 6 5 4
Library of Congress Cataloging-in-Publication Data
Wilder-Taylor, Stefanie.
Naptime is the new happy hour : and other ways toddlers turn your life upside down / by Stefanie Wilder-Taylor.—1st ed.
p. cm.
ISBN-13: 978-1-4169-5413-2
ISBN-10: 1-4169-5413-9
1. Motherhood—Humor. 2. Mothers—Humor. 3. Parent and child—Humor. 4. Mothers—Life skills guides. I. Title.
HQ759.W499 2008
306.874'30973—dc22
2007046881

In memory of my father, Stanley Myron Handelman—
and his subtle, silly sense of humor

ACKNOWLEDGMENTS

A debt of gratitude to my entire hardworking team at Simon Spotlight Entertainment, especially the ballsy and beautiful Jennifer Bergstrom, the amazingly hardworking and well-connected Jennifer Robinson, and, of course, my editor, Patrick Price, who hears my voice and makes it clearer and who also coined my favorite new phrase, "multitasking paper products." Thanks to all of you for making me feel I'm part of a family. And to Michael Broussard (calm down, I was just getting to you): None of this would have happened if it weren't for you! Good eye!

I would also like to thank my agent, Andrea Barzvi, for being warm and whip smart, always having my back, and never acting too "agenty."

Thanks to my friends Irene Zutell, Kimberly Prince, and Brian Frazer, who took time to read chapters, give great notes, and tell me to "just finish the damn book already!"

To Lisa Sundstedt—heeeeeeeeeeeeeello, Irene (again), Lara Tochner, Dani Klein, Kimberly (again), Julie Kasem, and Shannon Kennedy for putting up with all my neuroses and/or letting me exploit their lives.

To the greatest doctors, my pediatrician, Dr. Peter Schulman, and my rockstar OB, Dr. Rebecca Perlow (great job for your first time).

To Margaret Laysha and the entire staff of Elby's incredible preschool, Sage Academy, thank you.

There isn't ever a big enough bonus to properly thank Andrea Lockhart for always taking the best care of my daughter while I slaved away writing (okay, playing online poker) and never once reporting me to Social Services. You rock!

A quick shout-out to Eric and the whole staff at My Gym Encino for being such an awesome place to take my kid every Thursday. Also, thanks to Jessica Denay and Michelle Fryer at Hot Moms Club for being so great, flexible, and understanding while I finished this book.

To my second editor and brother, Michael Wilder: Your help, your hilarious jokes, and your friendship, as always, have been absolutely invaluable. I'm so grateful to you for everything. And to my sister-in-law, Racquel, let's just drop the "in-law" at this point, shall we?

To the inspiration behind this book: my beautiful, sassy, smart muse, my daughter Elby. Just when I think I couldn't love you more, I do. And lastly, my husband, my best friend, my fantasy football partner, Jon—I couldn't have done this or anything else in life without you. Nor would I ever want to. Thank you for loving me more than I deserve, doing way more than your share, and making me a mother.

Contents

Naptime Really *Is* the New Happy Hour

Being a mom is the hardest job you'll ever love. Don't you hate it when people try to pass these kind of bullshit platitudes off as inspirational? Because yes, it is a job. And yes, you will often enjoy it. But mostly, you'll love your child more than you could have imagined in your wildest mothering fantasies—but not necessarily the actual work involved. From potty training to researching a preschool that won't eat up your food budget for the year, to being forced to differentiate between a couple of cookies and a cookie binge, parenting a toddler is a 24/7 business that leaves little time for mellow evenings out with your husband, watching television that isn't animated, or even a quick phone chat with a girlfriend.

Regardless of whether you go to work, stay at home, or work at home, you (like me and countless other moms) will find yourself living for that occasion you can socialize, do your thing, really let your hair down—that at least two-hour (if you're lucky), guilt-free window that is yours and yours alone. Yes, naptime really is the new happy hour.

Whether or not for you "naptime" falls in the middle of the day or after the kids are finally in bed, this is the time you'll finally be able to have that bottle of wine, pay your bills, and update your Netflix queue. Who am I kidding? Personally, I usually don't have the mental power to microwave a baked potato, let alone figure out which DVDs I'll be interested in watching for the next month. But chances are you're more ambitious than I am—hell, Sheetrock is more ambitious than I am at this point. But no matter what you do with your time, it's only when the kids are asleep that you officially get to punch out.

You thought it would be different, right? You thought once the first deliriously draining, sleep-deprived, sex-deprived first year was behind you, you would get back to some semblance of normalcy, right? Not so fast there, my friend. In fact, let's all have a good laugh at how delusional we were.

I too believed mothers who told tales of their two-year-old who got up, made herself a bowl of cereal, and watched TV on her own while Mama slept in until the soul-recharging hour of eight thirty. I waited for that day—I held on—but it never came to pass. The truly sad part is, it doesn't even matter now, because suddenly I wake up *on my own* at seven a.m.! What the hell? I thought only senior citizens drained of every ounce of their body's melatonin started naturally waking up that early. Next thing you know I'll be relaxing with a cup of Sanka, driving forty-five miles per hour on the freeway with my blinker on, and heading over to Coco's for the early bird special.

Wait, I *have* been to Coco's for the early bird special . . . this is worse than I thought. Let's face it, the all-consuming nature of parenting can't help but change you.

For the first year your main job in the parenting biz is to keep the little suckers alive. Now that's not nearly enough. A mom of a toddler has a whole new set of concerns, worries, and questions, like "Who the hell is this Dora chick? And why does my child need to own everything with her picture on it?" "Is it wrong to have a cocktail at two in the afternoon?" And "Where did my child learn to say 'shit'?" Where's the book for that?

You have way more responsibility now. You're shaping little minds, imparting valuable lessons like, "Just because your mom eats food off the floor, doesn't mean you can do it. Mama has specially designed antibacterial stomach enzymes that have the ability to kill germs. Do you understand?" It's a lot of pressure. Your every move is under a microscope, and whatever you do or say will reverberate through the rest of your child's life! Are you dialing your therapist yet?

If that wasn't enough, you now have to navigate the treacherous waters known as "other moms" if you ever hope for your child to have a social life outside of his friends on *Sesame Street*. I once endured a mind-numbing playdate with a French woman who tried to engage me in a heated debate over the subtle difference between Ziploc *storage* bags and Ziploc *freezer* bags all afternoon. What's French for "Please kill me now"? Those are three hours I'll never have back. But boredom can be a holiday compared to spending time with the judgy moms who will stare you down as you hand your child a third Oreo as if you just tossed a dry-cleaning bag into their crib.

But here's the good news: Parenting a toddler is also a lot more rewarding. Baby milestones may seem exciting at the time; the first time your baby rolls over you may want to call everyone in your electronic address book, and when your baby takes his first steps you will be tempted to send out a professional press release. And if you're one of those tedious people who insists on commemorating each and every infant first with a full photo collage, you will be kept extremely busy. With babies, the firsts just keep on coming: first taste of strained peaches, subsequent first spit-up on your brand-new infant car seat cover, first time sleeping through the night, first emergency call to Poison Control, first trip to the ER, first visit from Social Services—I agree the year between zero and one is chock-full of exciting firsts.

But if you can believe it, toddler milestones feel even more monumental. There was something about seeing my daughter riding her little Radio Flyer tricycle for the first time that made me want to stuff her back in my womb and refuse to let her ever leave the safety of my body again—but not before filling an entire digital memory card with pictures.

The biggest difference between baby and toddler landmarks is that with babies we're mostly onlookers, waiting for our tiny charges to decide they're man enough to take those first steps. We're not officially part of the process. Our only job seems to be making sure we don't drop the two-thousand-dollar video camera. But unless toddlers have their own credit card, they are at the mercy of our good judgment when it comes to drinking out of a cup without safety handles and a spout, exchanging diapers for *My Little Pony* underpants, or leaving the comfort of the crib for the vast wasteland known as the big-girl bed. Plus, even if they managed to finagle a little cash from Grandma, there'd still be the issue of a finding a ride to the nearest Target or Ikea, so it's safe to say, at this point, we're still in charge.

But how *does* one determine when it's time to let our babies move forward? How do you decide when to move to the big bed or when to let your child drink from a real cup? And just a warning: If you think potty training leaves a lot of wet floors, you ain't seen nothin' yet. I found that a toddler and a cup with no lid should never ever be free to roam around a living room, unless you have an extremely low deductible on your home insurance or at the bare minimum, stain-resistant carpets. But much like potty training, it's up to you to decide when and if you're ready. By the number of eight-year-olds I see with normal wrist control running around sporting their colorful spouted mugs, some parents are *never* ready. I started offering my daughter a regular cup as early as she could hold it, but it wasn't until recently that my nerves calmed down considerably; mainly because her balance is finally perfected enough to bring me a glass of wine without spilling.

Not to sound like a big fat tired-ass cliché but, my God, these babies do grow up fast. Before you know it, your big-boy-bed-sleepin', Curious-George-underpants-wearin', regular-size-cup-drinking little person who may or may not have given up their blankie will be ready for the biggest, most gut-wrenching, bittersweet milestone of all, his first day of preschool. For this one, you'd be wise to buy stock in Kleenex, because you will both be crying—and not just from the price!

Raising a child is life altering and heart melting for even the toughest cynic. I should know—I went through some of these changes kicking and screaming. I never thought I'd ever in a *million years* have to say this, but I'm currently shopping minivans. I cried when I first realized I'd be going down that road, but there's some serenity to realizing that I'm a mother and it's okay. I'm not as cool as I once thought I was, but who cares? This life is more fun than I ever thought possible. And even when I do get the van, don't worry, I will not deck it out with two dozen bumper stickers, drive around with that requisite day-old, half-empty McDonald's Diet Coke in the cup holder, or try to bring fanny packs and a visor back into style as so many minivan owners seem to do. Okay, fine! I'll probably drive around with the old Diet Coke, but that's it. What are you going to do? That's all part of being a mother—or as my daughter says, "Thaaaat's Elmo's World. . . ."

Part One: Your New and Improved but Strangely Less Exciting Life

Suburban Boredom

When I moved from funky Santa Monica to L.A.'s snoozy San Fernando Valley, it was while I was pregnant, and my husband and I were hoping to find a nice, safe community to raise our offspring. The goal was to buy a house we could afford without moving across the country to do it. We were moving from a place where homeless men made bonfires in my garage and the middle-aged guy who cut hair down the street at Fantastic Sam's also sold bongs. But the coffee shop on our block had been there for thirty years, and there were ten used record stores in a two-mile radius, so it was a bittersweet farewell.

I thought for sure we'd found the right house and neighborhood when we took a six p.m. drive to see it after reading the ad on the Internet. There, in front of our potential new house, was a four-year-old boy tooling around on a scooter. The only four-year-old child in our own 'hood had a rat tail and a Barney tattoo. I knew we were onto something. We returned to the new house the next day, offer in hand. The sale went through, and we were quickly on our way to suburban bliss.

The moving trucks may have taken us only ten miles from our old apartment, but as we quickly discovered, we may as well have crossed the equator. The honeymoon period didn't last long.

Suburbia. It's only ten miles from Hollywood Boulevard, but trust me, no one here is taking any day trips to the Wax Museum, although many of the locals could pass for an exhibit there. We found our new environment disconcerting at best. The women here seemed completely different from the people I was used to. They were all mommies. Conservative mommies. These were women who had more than hairstyles, they had hairdos. These people and I were a world apart. I was stopped on the street and inundated with information about food allergies, problem elementary schools, and which Ralph's grocery store sold fresher produce—things I had absolutely no interest in.

Given the fact that I was pregnant and sick, I had the perfect excuse to avoid most of them and the outside world altogether. I spent the majority of my days enjoying my picturesque new neighborhood from the safety of my couch. When my daughter came, I found I had little time to attend book club, let alone read the book (which always featured a heroine who lived in the fourteenth century), and turned down offers to play Bunco, some sort of suburban version of Yahtzee, based on the fear that I couldn't pronounce it correctly.

But as my baby grew older, I knew I'd have to try and

acclimate if she was ever going to have a friend who lived in walking distance. Plus, I was starting to need some local friends of my own, since I was too lazy to actually drive to any of the ones I already had.

A "better late than never" opportunity came to me in the form of an Evite to a Pampered Chef party. I had no idea what that involved, but how bad could it be? The word "pampered" was right in the name! And it was held after my kid would be safely in bed but within a block of my house, which translated loosely into "unrestricted drinking." I was in.

I had no idea this tiny step down the street was actually a giant step into the world of Home Parties for stay-at-home moms—whom I soon came to know by their acronym (SAHMs)—who want to start their own pyramid scheme businesses, including Pampered Chef (think Amway with the reps all wielding sharp paring knives). I am one of those who feel extremely uncomfortable and obligated when faced with anyone trying to sell me something. I've learned to live with my disability—I keep my distance from car lots and cosmetic counters and refrain from opening my front door to little hoodlums who are trying to stay out of gangs by selling me a tiny box of caramel chocolate turtles for ten bucks. I find it extraordinarily difficult to say, "No, thank you," so these kinds of parties are less than ideal places for me.

I walked in, naively hopeful and with a "let the pampering begin" positive attitude! I plopped down among my fellow partygoers, who were actual eager participants, perused my very own Pampered Chef brochure, and scoped out the small crowd for someone to talk to. But before any neighborly exchanges could start, the demonstration was underway. A green-aproned woman in charge of our group took center stage and apologized way too many times that this was her first time leading a Pampered Chef party and how she was filling in for a much more experienced Pampered Chef leader but that her lack of knowledge certainly wouldn't stop her from pressuring us to buy an array of unnecessary appliances.

It was dawning on me that there would be no mani/pedis, martinis, or even culinary delicacies. I realized that other than a glass of Two-Buck Chuck Chablis, I wasn't going to be offered much in the way of pampering—unless you consider being presented a way to clear out my pesky bank account by purchasing overpriced kitchen gadgets as pampering.

I morosely gazed at a glossy photo of a forty-five-dollar can opener whose main feature seemed to be that it leaves the can's top edges smooth. *What purpose does this serve?* I wondered. *Is it so you won't slice your hand open while reaching into the trash to retrieve those cookies you tossed away prematurely?*

I glanced around and noticed that not a single person looked put off by the poverty-inducing prices and were marking costly mango slicers and barbecue tongs with fervor—not unlike born-again Christians at a Bible study circling their favorite passages. I started to sweat a little bit and felt a definite lack of oxygen in the room. I didn't belong here. I didn't own a minivan, I couldn't keep up my end of a conversation about granite countertops, and my kitchen was the size of a walk-in closet. The safety of my own house was only a few paces away, but it might as well have been a hundred miles—I knew I was not getting out of here without at least purchasing a thirty-dollar wooden spoon.

It wasn't like I didn't try. At one lull in the demonstration, I attempted to strike up a quiet conversation with the woman seated next to me on the couch. In her cat-eye glasses she looked an awful lot like the singer Lisa Loeb, and she'd brought a delightful three-level bean dip, so I figured her a candidate for best friendship. Unfortunately, I couldn't move the chat away from the dip without completely losing her interest. But I pushed forward anyway.

"What do you do?" I asked, pretending that networking at a Pampered Chef party was completely natural for me.

"I'm in the music business," she answered, barely glancing up from her brochure.

In this part of town that could have meant anything. She could have conducted the Philharmonic nightly at the Hollywood Bowl or led the sing-along at Gymboree on Thursday afternoons.

"Oh, really?" I hoped she'd elaborate.

"Uh-huh." No such luck. She was deeply involved in scoring some Corn Cob Nobs.

"This dip truly is delicious. I mean, look at me, I can't stop shoveling it in my face! Ha ha ha!"

I pulled out all the stops but got nowhere. I faked enthusiasm for a jewel-encrusted melon baller, hummed "Stay" under my breath, and finished off the bean dip, but the more I tried, the more I seemed to be scaring her. "Lisa" made a bigger space between us on the couch. *Who cares?* I thought. Why the hell was I wasting my time trying to befriend this Lisa Loeb wannabe when I could be saving my conversation gold for the off chance that someday I might meet the real Lisa Loeb? Apparently boredom was making me desperate.

I turned my attention back to our cult leader, who was in the midst of showing off a trifle bowl. It was at that point I started having violent thoughts toward Green Apron Lady. No matter how long I lived on this earth, let alone in the burbs, I would never need to know the definition of a trifle bowl. Plus, I feared that if I did find out, I would lose some truly valuable information in my brain, like my social security number. I had just come here to meet my neighbors. Was that so wrong?

Mercifully, the party came to a close before I had a chance to yell out any of the inappropriate thoughts going through my head. I planned to make a beeline for the exit, but as we all turned in our order sheets (I, in fact, ended up ordering the smooth-edge-making can opener—I would get to the bottom of it if I had to go bankrupt trying), a few women straggled behind to discuss the upcoming block party meeting. Block party meeting? Another chance to meet my neighbors! Much like labor pains, the horror of the Pampered Chef party was already starting to fade . . . and I jotted down the details.

It's true that I had to alter the original visions that had danced in my head of mutually supportive and independent-minded women on their front lawns enjoying a glass of vino while the kids played. Just by my initial judgment of the neighborhood women, drinking on your front lawn would seem frowned upon. But I adjusted my expectations and continued to make an effort. Later I found out fun is still had, only furtively—bottles of wine were hidden in someone's backyard during the block party while a code was handed from cool mom to cool mom directing her where to find the secret contraband.

Not that drinking was so high on my agenda. I mean, yes, I've enjoyed a glass of wine or three while watching my child play with other children. And sure, some may judge. But judge away. My kid enjoys my personality when I'm one-sheet-to-the-wind. Let's put it this way: I'd give a much worse impromptu puppet show sober. But please, before you start writing me hate mail, I don't think you should get drunk around a child *ever*—unless, of course, they're drunk too. You don't want to make your kid drink alone. That's just mean. And may give your child a complex.

Ever so slowly I did become acclimated to my suburban surroundings. Although I still didn't play Bunco, I learned how to say it, and I was actually starting to fit in. At the neighborhood Halloween party (at which I ran the face-painting booth), I saw the woman who had generously invited me to the Pampered Chef party and stopped her to talk. Something was still on my mind.

"Hey, Janet, I think I may have come on a little strong to that one chick in the cat-eye glasses at your Pampered Chef party."

"Oh, you mean Lisa Loeb? I manage her! She's really such a doll!" God, I should have known it was the real Lisa Loeb when I noticed she'd ordered the Cheese Bistro Set and Sandwich Crimper, which had to have cost more than my Volvo.

Thanks to Janet, the suburbs were looking up.

"Interesting. Do you think she'll be at the next Pampered Chef party?" I said, trying my very best not to sound like a stalker.

"Probably," she said, moving away from me. *Yes!*

"Well, see ya there, neighbor! Save me a spoon rest!"

Oh, the Places You'll Go! (Or Won't)

I'm just going to say it: It's a bitch to stay home with a pre-preschool-age child all day. We have very different agendas. It seems that they want to do stuff all the time, and I, well, don't want to do stuff ever. But we need to meet them in the middle, right? Isn't that what parenting is all about? Basically, having a toddler is exactly like hosting an out-of-town guest . . . indefinitely. You pretty much feel like cruise director Julie from *The Love Boat* (minus the off-camera cocaine addiction). Every day is the same as "your guest" awakens, waiting to be entertained.

"So, would you like to watch some Elmo?"

"No."

Despite the fact that you're already low on ideas and have not a drop of caffeine in you yet, you know she is waiting for your next offer, and it better be fantastic!

"So are you still keeping up with that *Dora the Explorer*?" Nothin'.

"Okay, why don't I just leave the remote next to you and I'll see about breakfast. How about a waffle?"

"Okay."

Uh-oh. Spoke too soon. "Shoot. Sweetie, we're out of waffles."

"Want a waffle!" followed by thirty seconds of hearty sobs. Just like an out-of-town guest! And like any guest who doesn't know her surroundings, your child is depending on you to show her a good time. The pressure is always on to make each and every day count. There's no period where she goes home and you lay on the couch watching E! for a couple of days, unwinding from the constant activity until you start to miss her and begin to plan her next trip to the coast.

If you're going to get through the years before your child is in preschool full-time without developing a drug addiction or *worse* drug addiction, you'll need to lower your expectations of what constitutes an exciting day for your child. I know too many women who spend an inordinate amount of time looking for fun and educational things to do with their kid *every day*. Planetarium? That new exotic animal zoo that opened a mere three-hour car ride from your house? The opera? To me, this is pure psychosis.

I try to think of my child as a pint-size foreign exchange student: She barely speaks the language and everything in this country is pretty much new to her. While other mothers are planning their four-hour excursion to the aviation museum, my kid's having a blast at the Sprint store.

I'm not saying *never* go on any of these ambitious field trips, just space them out. Remember, it's not the entertainment Olympics, although your fellow teammates would have you believe otherwise.

I have this crafty friend, Susan (you know the type; if she were 10 percent less cool she'd be scrapbooking) who guilted me into going to this arts and crafts studio. For five bucks an hour your kid can screw around with paint and glitter and feathers like a miniature Bob Mackie in training. The downside is, you have to watch them every second or your day may be cut short by some sort of glue gun tragedy. Susan bought a one-year membership for fifty dollars. I didn't buy the membership. We only went one more time. Guess who's up forty bucks?

You just need an activity to bridge the gap to their next period of sleep. My rule of thumb is, don't go anywhere you have to MapQuest.

There is a magical land, probably three exits from your house, just waiting to help you burn off two hours— similar to Disneyland but minus the hundred dollars in admission fees: TARGET! Target's like catnip to moms. Sure, I enjoyed running out to Target every once in a while before I had a baby; but now I can't get enough. The Target experience starts with the ease of the parking lot, because all the spaces are so huge. It's almost like it's all handicapped parking. And really, isn't having a small child a teeny bit of a handicap?

Then there are the wide, beckoning electric doors,

which *open* for you automatically. At the mall, you could grow a beard standing in front of the door to Macy's, pushing a stroller and adjusting forty pounds of diaper bag from shoulder to shoulder while people give you a "hey, it was your decision to have a kid" look and pass you by. When I become mayor, I will make it mandatory to open doors for women with strollers. Violators will be forced to listen to the *Elmo's World* theme song on an endless loop. Yes, I will be *that* strict!

Now where was I? The Target dollar bins. Unless you are a parent or over eighty years old, you'll have no interest in this area. But in my experience, it's better than Splenda. On a recent trip, I found my daughter some puffy plastic flower stickers. She immediately proceeded to completely cover her arms and legs with them—which is totally something I would do now! It was so darn cute I was wishing that we were on security camera so she could be discovered by a security guard/talent scout. Don't judge, it *is* Los Angeles.

While my daughter entertains herself with her one-dollar babysitter, I am free to wander aimlessly from section to section, imagining all the ways Target could help me make my house a home, if only I had the slightest decorating savvy whatsoever. Sadly, I can't accessorize, don't know squat about thread count, and wouldn't know a canapé if it bit me on the ass. It's true; I don't have a gay man's bone in my body. But I have a rich fantasy life.

Finally I try to slip past the toy section to avoid my daughter accidentally seeing something with a picture of Dora emblazoned on it, causing her to start screaming "buy it" until I want to cut my ear off with a pair of safety scissors I bought for a buck. Going home is the saddest part. I'm putting my exhausted, nap-ready peanut into the hot car only to find I've left her damn sippy cup at home and now she's softly sobbing "cup." But I don't blame Target for that, just myself. And hell, when we get home we'll probably spend some quality time in the blow-up pool, which I scored at, you guessed it, Target for $9.99! Yes! One morning down, five hundred seventy-two to go.

Other Good Places To Take Your Child Within a Few Miles from Your House

The Bookstore—Think of a bookstore as a giant maze with all the shelves as secret passages. Also, think of those secret passages as a way for your kid to get lost. Once, when my daughter was about sixteen months old, I put her down and turned my back for a split second, and when I turned back around she had completely disappeared. The next five minutes spent racing through the aisles felt like twenty straight heart attacks. And having to ask a manager to block the front doors because my child was on the loose didn't make my Top Ten Proudest Mom Moments. Finally the manager found her laying down under a *Where the Wild Things Are* poster and brought her back to me. We go to a different bookstore now.

But bookstores also have a giant—and luckily barely supervised—kids' area. This is where your little one can hug, kiss, and slobber on stuffed animals, refuse to actually open any book, disrupt the "story time reader," tear a page out of a magazine, and help themselves to some crayons that you haven't paid for. Children's bookstores are even better, because they rarely press charges. Overall, I find this to be a good way to spend an hour.

The Grocery Store—If you want to get your errands done while entertaining your child, let your kid ride in the basket of the cart. I realize it says right on the cart that kids must be in the seat, blah blah, safety hazard, blah. No kid I know will sit still that way while you analyze the subtle differences in ingredients between Skippy and Jif. Stick 'em in the basket and go really fast. Just don't knock over any displays or the cashier may refuse to give out a balloon or lollipop—which will be the whole reason your child agreed to go with you in the first place.

And don't forget about the filthy rides in front of drugstores and supermarkets. I've known kids who just like to stare at them for a half hour. Okay, my kid. And yes, I've had her tested. It's normal! And might I add, quite the money saver. And that half hour is the perfect opportunity to read the *National Enquirer* you bought so you don't have to bring it home and get made fun of by your husband.

The 99 Cents Store—Even if your child runs around the aisles breaking crap for a half hour, you'll still ending up spending less than what you would on a Happy Meal. For a good laugh, have your child ask every salesclerk, "How much is this?" The employees won't find it amusing at all, which will make it all the more entertaining for you.

Crafts Stores—Personally, and I may have mentioned this already, I'm not the crafty type; I don't even like the cut-and-paste feature on my WordPerfect computer program. But kids are highly entertained by a crafts store, and I love an entertained kid. Boy and girl children alike will browse colorful beads, construction paper, and ready-to-paint figurines with more enthusiasm than a starlet browsing Oscar de la Renta's collection for a dress to wear to the Emmys. The great thing about these shops is you can buy your kid a bargain rubber stamp and inkpad for a buck fifty and score another two hours of distraction from it back at home. And that's not including the three hours it will take to wash "Grandma's Numero Uno" off of every surface of their little body.

The Park—Children are like puppies. They need to run and jump and trek sand and poop into your house. The park is a must. Don't bother lugging a bucket, shovel, and other toys, because your child will act like anything that belongs to him/her is kryptonite, while anything that another kid plays with is just the exact thing they need!

Remember, you are doing this for your child, and they are having fun, despite the highly irritating conversation you may be overhearing. Like the one where a woman with a face too wide for a bob haircut may have said, "I had to fire Maria, my cleaning lady. I came home yesterday and she had 'forgotten' to clean my microwave," and the other women may have actually nodded in sympathy. And then Face Too Wide for a Bob Haircut may have gone on to say, "I've recommended Maria to all of my friends. I think she's cleaning *too* many houses, and since she's getting more business and more money, she's gotten lazy." More sympathy nods. "I guess I'm partially to blame. I'm too nice." And then I *may* have said something under my breath to Face Too Fucking Wide for a Bob Haircut like, "I seriously doubt anything in your life is the result of you being too nice," which *may* have escalated into a verbal altercation and me not being able to return to that particular park for a few weeks. But you will probably have a great time.

Anywhere with Trains—Kids love 'em. I don't get it. But I don't need to. Real trains, fake trains, the smell of trains, the rock group Train. Whatever—it's all good fun to a toddler.

A Few Places That Seem Like a Good Idea, but Trust Me, They're Not

Indoor Playgrounds—First of all, I have never seen one of these places that contained a toy or piece of equipment bought more recently than a Members Only jacket. The air always has that vague dirty diaper smell, and since they only break out the Lysol on special occasions, you'll spend the whole time wondering if the smell is wafting off your kid. For some reason there are always two of the rowdiest, most obnoxious eight-year-old boys, with no parents in sight, constantly running up to you shouting, "I have a dinosaur!" And shockingly, there seem to be no noise restrictions in these hellholes, so unless you're *trying* to get a migraine for some reason, I'd avoid these places like a Kevin Federline concert.

The Mall—In the first year, your infant may sit in a stroller while you browse for things you can't afford because YOU HAVE A BABY and wouldn't fit into anyway because YOU JUST HAD A BABY. But once they're upright and mobile, you're screwed, and good luck going anywhere except the play area—always conveniently located next to a Mrs. Fields, like my ass isn't big enough already. And with the apparent lack of cleaning happening, the kids may as well be playing in a bus station bathroom. Your child is practically guaranteed to come home with something for which there's no known vaccine.

Crate & Barrel—Just . . . NO. Do I really have to tell you not to take a child here? If so, put the book down and walk away. Same goes for Pottery Barn, the Sharper Image and, obviously, anyplace that sells sunglasses.

Toy Stores—Unless you have a hundred thousand dollars lying around or you're dying to use the word NO a hundred thousand times, stay out of toy stores while your child is in tow. Not that going to a toy store without your child is fun either. Unless your idea of a good time is listening to *other* parents say no a hundred thousand times to their crying children. Word to the weary: Shop online.

Blackjack Tables—Hanging out in a smoky casino with a toddler all day may *seem* like just the thing, but it's not, for one main reason: Toddlers are notorious for hitting on sixteen when the dealer is showing a four.

Police Stations—Why tempt fate?

Halloween—and Other Holidays You May End Up Hating Less Than You Thought

Once you were above the age of sixteen, and before you had a child, if you were anything like me, you'd rather have had a gig as the ball-pit cleaner at Chuck E. Cheese than celebrate Halloween or brave the mall anytime in the months preceding Christmas. Just wait. It's funny how your perspective shifts when these holidays are seen though the eyes of your toddler. Suddenly the question "What are you going to be for Halloween?" doesn't cause choking, even if it's asked in July.

I'm going to 'fess up about something. It's time to come clean and lay it out there for you. Okay, here it is: I get so excited for Halloween now I can hardly stand it. Starting around September, I feel like Matt Perry with a big bottle of Vicodin in front of him. Or me with a big bottle of Vicodin, for that matter. Why is this a big deal? Because I have proudly despised Halloween and all of its time-wasting, humiliating traditions since I first became too old to go trick-or-treating without drawing odd stares.

Sure, when I was young and dumb and ready to get blotto on sugar for the week or so following the festivities, it was all good. Although even back then I didn't express much creativity in the costume department. Every year I was a witch, except for the one year I decided to shake things up. I was a wizard—same dress, different hat. My younger brother and I would trek through our suburban Spokane neighborhood, gleefully yelling, "Trick or treat!" even at the old crabby people's houses with no lights on and not a pumpkin in sight, who clearly wanted no part of us.

Once we got back to the house, the bartering would begin. In my favor was the fact that my brother had no sweet tooth—doesn't to this day. What the hell is wrong with a person who can take or leave *candy*? It's sort of like alcohol. In my opinion, you should either like to drink or abstain completely because you used to like to drink *waaaay* too much. But these "just never liked the taste of it" teetotaler types make me suspicious. Don't they have any feelings they need to repress? So the candy wheeling and dealing went down pretty uneventfully. I would trade him some of those lame, soft, orange circus-peanut things for fifteen mini Almond Joys. Then I would throw a couple of Smarties his way in exchange for some mini Razzles, Bottle Caps, and candy corn.

For the next three months, I would raid his stash slowly but surely, because he ate it at the snail-on-downers pace of one piece per day. Eventually I'd leave him with a few pineapple Dum Dum lollipops, and he wouldn't even notice until the following year.

Then I got older. And once the trick-or-treating, candy-gorging portion of my childhood was over, what was left? Nothing. Sewing a costume? Not for this girl. Thinking up something really clever to wear with my boyfriend? What, so we could be John and Lorena Bobbitt! Ha ha ha! No. Every All Hallows' Eve since I owned my first training bra, I'd hide out in my room with the lights off, having turned down the all-too-common invite to a costume party. The images of my friends (or worse, coworkers) dressed as the slutty nurse, the slutty kitty, or the slutty unicorn were ones I needed to avoid.

Thank God that when I met my future husband, I found out he felt the exact same way. We became Halloween Scrooges together, avoiding the people who loved to dress up, rolling our eyes at fake spiderweb-covered trees and other insanely over-the-top decorations that covered the front lawns of our neighborhood. We took a pass on each and every invite to "come over and watch scary movies and make popcorn and hand out treats to the kids!"

So what happened? The kid happened. And it will happen to you if it hasn't already.

It all started when my mom friend Crafty Susan offered to loan me a costume for our then two-year-old daughter. "I'm not sure we're into that . . ." was my first response. She'd bought about thirty of them on sale and insisted that I "just take a look." And then she lobbied to "just have her try one on." Then she pinched my arm. So, to stop the pain (and because she offered to make spinach artichoke dip), I agreed.

And then I saw it. The Bumblebee. Oh yeah, little stinger, puffy little body, netted wings, bouncing antennae—she looked like a little John Belushi circa 1975! I almost shed a tear. You know what she said when she had this on? "I'zz a bee." Um-hmm.

And that's when I became a big old Halloween whore.

We went trick-or-treating, and it was just like I'd never stopped. Crafty Susan's two-year-old giraffe and my little bee stopped at every house in the neighborhood, even the ones with no decorations or lights on—especially those—and brought home a huge stash of treats, which I slowly pilfered for old time's sake. We practically broke our cameras from taking so many pictures.

Since then it's been, "Bring on the costumes. Bring on the candy, jack-o'-lanterns, roasted pumpkin seeds, skeletons that hang from the front door (okay, maybe not that—that requires actually hanging stuff up). Bring on the trick-or-treating and bring on the SPIRIT OF HALLOWEEN!" And by the way, the spirit of Halloween does not include giving out little bags of raisins as a "healthy alternative." You know who you are, and if you do it again next year, you will find your house toilet-papered, my friend!

Of course, the moment Halloween is done, we're up early ironing our flags for Veterans Day! Having kids is all about holidays, and Halloween is just the tip of the festivities iceberg. I have found that no matter what your religious persuasion, holidays can become fun again for all families.

Christmas

Please don't judge me, but I'm a Jew who celebrates Christmas. I used to take pride in my lack of holiday sentimentality, my refusal to take part in the commercialized season, but that false front really does get left by the wayside when you see the look on your sweetie's face Christmas morning. I haven't taken it to the make-my-own Christmas cards level that many mommies do the second they're knocked up. And I can assure you, even if I outdo the Duggar family and have eighteen kids, I still will never send out a mass Christmas letter/update on the mundane lives of the "Taylor Family" (those get round-filed as soon as I take them out of the mailbox). But I'm certainly not above waiting in line for my daughter to sit on Santa's lap. Sure, I'm aware that most store Santas likely possess a criminal record, but I figure, hey, I'm not hiring the guy to be my nanny. Plus, maybe that's my own baggage.

I will say that my fear of fellow grown-ups in costumes does extend much further than Halloween. I've always had a deep mistrust of the Disney characters walking around the theme park. Who knows who's in that Goofy costume? It could be any weirdo who can't get a real job. That big plushy may look innocent enough, but how do I know that while posing for that digital photo, Tigger's not going to try and touch my boob? I'm not risking it. But my daughter's a different story. She loves them all; the insane-looking giant Easter Bunny, Homeless Santa, the Jolly Green Giant, whatever, she'll walk right up to them at the mall and plop down on their lap. Meanwhile I'm quivering behind, eating a Wetzel's pretzel and trying to avoid any human-to-character eye contact.

No matter what you celebrate, the main thing to remember around this time of year is the true spirit of the holiday season. And, of course, I'm talking about presents. All kids love the concept of presents. But remember, before you go and spend an inordinate amount of money on toys, your toddler will only be interested in them about as long as it takes you to figure out what's on TV that night. This is where relatives come in. During the toddler years, most kids don't have a really good handle on exactly what they want for Christmas/Hanukkah/Kwanzaa/December. Take full advantage of this! A big pile of gifts is a big pile of gifts, no matter whether they came from you, Aunt Penny, or the 99 cents store.

A good rule of thumb is that you should spend more on wrapping paper than you do on presents. Trust me, it'll take them more time to unwrap the present than to break it. My daughter loved the Dora cash register she got for Christmas last year, which set her father and me back about twenty bucks, but she was equally thrilled with an old pinecone she found in the driveway that same morning. Keep that in mind before spending your week's grocery money on a two-minute distraction.

An entertaining and relatively inexpensive part of this holiday is the tree. Despite my Jewish-Christmas-loving status, before having a baby I'd never actually bought a Christmas tree. It seemed like a lot of work, getting that tree home, carting it in and out of the house—especially since I'd never owned a bungee cord. I knew I'd end up as one of those people who just left the tree up all year round because it was too much trouble to drag its rotting carcass out to the curb. But once my daughter was here, it started sounding more and more like a must-have.

For the first couple of years, foliage plus electricity in your living room probably isn't the greatest plan. But once your baby reaches toddler status, go for it, 'cause trimming the tree will possibly be the highlight of the season.

Last year we got one of those Advent calendars to help our daughter count down to Christmas. She would open a little door each day in December, eat a piece of chocolate, and run around high on sugar for forty-five minutes jabbering about Santa Claus. It was so cute. It kind of reminded me of how excited I get the month before I'm due for a cell phone upgrade.

If you're the type of person who starts your holiday shopping in June, makes all your own ornaments, considers scrapbooking a great night, goes to a crafts store "just to browse," and has ever signed up for an origami class, we'll probably never be friends, but we can definitely agree on one thing: Holidays make parenting fun.

More Holiday Fun

Easter—Does anyone else get a tingle in their groin when the grocery store registers start to put out those cream-filled Cadbury eggs? What other holiday practically force-feeds you chocolate and marshmallows—can I get a *whoop-whoop*? And the best part is, this holiday isn't just fun for adults; children love it too! Easter egg hunts are a great way to entertain kids for an hour, but they do require an inordinate amount of organization and planning. A good time- and money-saver is to get up early, head over to a neighbor's house, and have your kids find *their* meticulously decorated eggs and candy. Just make sure you're not wearing high heels, so you can get the hell out of there when they call the cops. Hey, I'm here to help.

Fourth of July—Fireworks probably lost their appeal for you after the age of ten, but the joy will be back with a vengeance when you have a child. Kids love sparkly things, fire, loud noises, hot dogs, and staying up past their bedtime. Every July fourth they'll feel they've hit the jack-pot! And every July fourth that no one loses a digit, you can feel like *you've* hit the jackpot! Really, the only member of the family who won't love this holiday is your dog, so pay extra attention to your pooch on his birthday.

Thanksgiving—First off, Thanksgiving takes on new meaning when you have a child; mainly because you get to exact payback for all the years you were forced to do time at the kids' table. Make sure you invite other family members with young children to share in the fun of setting up the card table and making the whole lot of them entertain one another by squirting yams between their teeth and fighting over the wishbone. Meanwhile, if you're lucky enough to not be hosting the big event, you can further revel in your adulthood by spending the entire day watching football, even if you've never watched a minute of it in your life; it's your God-given right! If you are having the big day at your house, try to farm out as many side dishes to child-free friends and relatives as you possibly can, leaving yourself on turkey and coffee duty only. And if you buy your turkey pre-made, I won't tell a soul.

Groundhog Day—Obviously one of the biggest drinking holidays of the year. But you knew that. If the groundhog sees his shadow, it's two more months of hardcore binge drinking. If not, same thing.

Less Holiday Fun

Unfortunately, there are a few holidays that, even if they were great at one point in your life, are best to be avoided now that you're a parent.

Valentine's Day—No other holiday has more potential for disaster than this one, where you are sure to hurt someone's feelings before the day is through. Men are lucky that CVS is open twenty-four hours, because otherwise you wouldn't even get that Whitman's Sampler and the Sudafed in the red box. Plus, sex won't be on the agenda, since you'll be too sleep deprived after staying up half the night before making cards for your kid's entire class. And after all your efforts, your little one will still come home crying because of another kid's less conscientious mother. This is where you pat yourself on the back for your superior parenting skills and then promptly pass out.

New Year's Eve—Every New Year's you will find yourself in the black hole of child care. Unless you want to fork out fifty bucks an hour for a sitter only to come home to find your good bottle of Andre Cold Duck champagne missing, you'll be staying home. The only resolution you will end up making is not to have any more children. It's best to leave this celebration to the young, dumb, and childless. Let them get a DUI while you lie on the couch, eat Chinese takeout, and try to figure out how many of Dick Clark's facial features are still original.

April Fools' Day—Has anyone ever in the history of time enjoyed having a practical joke played on them? I think the best April Fools' joke we can possibly play on our kids is to tell them that every April Fools' Day it's customary to buy our mother flowers and candy, and that night we all go to bed at seven.

Supermom or Superliar?

So there my daughter sits, sprawled out on a leather chair, eyes glazed over, fingers running OCD-style over her purple blanket, watching her fourth episode of Wonder Pets. I glace her way, wondering silently if I'm the worst mother on the planet for needing to get my bills paid (and read the latest on Paris Hilton) while not having my daughter interfere. Just a half hour, I tell myself, which inevitably turns into "One more episode, Mommy! Please!"

"No. I'm sorry, sweetie, but it's time to turn the television off and play outside for a while."

"I just want to watch a little more TV," she answers simply, quietly.

And I just want to read the Internet a little bit longer. It seems like a win-win situation, except for those pesky warnings about too much TV giving her ADD and liquefying her little still-forming brain. I imagine all the other moms who are at this moment coming up with some great project to do with their child or children, a project that involves gluing and glitter, cutting shapes out of construction paper, tracing the outline of a leaf, or even worse, *cavorting with nature.*

Maybe I should just stick a huge pile of cookies in front of her and a gallon of chocolate milk to wash down the Happy Meal she just ate. I silently berate myself while switching the TiVo to *Wonder Pets*, "Save the Pandas!" I glance back at my comatose toddler—is that drool coming off her chin? I want to slit my wrists out of guilt right now. But I don't. I finish paying my bills and try to find out why the latest celebrity coupling just broke up. Never far from my mind, though, is my daughter, who although happier than a gay man at a Cher concert, is obviously not getting the best of her mother.

This self-loathing moment has been brought to you by your local Smug Mama; those moms who will look you straight in the eye and say, "Oh, my child doesn't watch TV."

We're surrounded by them—moms who are busy trying to outdo one another's parenting on every level. Obviously, not every woman is like this. Most are mere mortals. But when faced with a self-proclaimed Supermom, you may not be able to help feeling like your parenting style is more on a par with Andrea Yates when reflected in their glow. But the thing to remember, the thing that will save you, is these women lie often. At the very least, their insecurities make them prone to major exaggeration.

When a man has the nerve to ask a woman how many sexual partners she's had, no matter what the woman says, the man tacks on at least five more, right? I actually think men are onto something. Hey, who among us hasn't shaved a one-night stand or four from our spotty sexual past? Guess what, women can utilize this trick in a different arena: the competitive, cutthroat mom sport of "I do everything better than you." I call this New Mommy Math, and you don't have to have passed algebra to master it; it's all about easy addition.

When Smug Mama tells you straight to your face that she absolutely allows only one hour of mind-enriching, educational TV a day, just go ahead and add two hours. If she tells you "No TV ever!" add six. It's that simple.

With this trick up your sleeve, you can decipher devious lying about sugar consumption, discipline, how much "household help" they utilize, cleaning, yelling, sex (not) having . . . and more! If you think you don't need my help, think again. Smug Mamas are everywhere, and they can strike at any time.

You'll be at the park having a perfectly great conversation with a real mom about breakfast cereal.

"God, remember Count Chocula? I used to live on that stuff."

"Oh yeah, but what ever happened to Boo Berry? The one with the ghost on the cover and the blue marshmallows? I haven't seen it since I was a kid!"

Suddenly Smug Mama will burst out from behind

a seesaw and blurt out, Tourette's-style, "Oh we would never let Dakota-Ryder eat sugary cereal. We're a sugar-free household. Dakota-Ryder-Banjo eats only All Bran No-Trace-of-Anything-That-Tastes-Remotely-Edible Flakes from Whole Foods. It's only eighty-five dollars a box."

Sounds good. Really. Gee, you got a coupon for that?

Your first reaction will possibly be to recall with horror that your son ate a Fruit Roll-Up and half a muffin (FINE, cupcake) for breakfast, and you'll feel terrible and less-than. But wait—stop—use your New Mommy Math. Bran Flakes my ass. Sure, Smug Mama may have offered that up, but no toddler who has working gums would let that soggy crap past his lips. She's lying. Go ahead and switch Bran Flakes to Corn Pops and you may be getting closer to the truth. Now add a few tablespoons of sugar sprinkled liberally on top, and you're probably somewhere in the actual vicinity. Feeling better?

Similarly, if Smug Mama tells you her child is allowed only two small cookies after dinner, feel safe adding five more. If she tells you no cookies, only fruit, go with eight. See? Now you're starting to get it. The formula is using the inverse—the more super the mom, the more super the liar.

My husband and I once went out of obligation to a function at a pseudo-friend's house for "adults" only. The host, a woman I never liked that much, was the mom of three rambunctious boys. There was expensive wine served and delightful canapés. It wasn't all bad. But the first thing I noticed was that the house was immaculate—not a Hot Wheel in sight. Of course, you know me; I couldn't keep my trap shut for a second.

"How do you do it? How can your house be this clean with three boys around? You actually have clean guest towels and no hair in your sink. I don't think my sink's been hairless since the early nineties. What's your secret?"

"I actually love cleaning. I clean every day anyway, so when a party comes up I'm already halfway there," Smug Mama responded with a fake smile.

I practically had an aneurysm on the spot. By the way, I should also tell you that this woman actually claims to enjoy making soups from scratch and loves to e-mail recipes and humorous chain mail with subject lines like *Why I Love My Girlfriends!* "I normally wouldn't send this kind of e-mail, but this one's really funny, you guys!!" She's the reason spam blocking was invented.

Out of necessity, I turned on my heel and headed for the bar to procure a much-needed flavored martini. Once the alcohol helped cleared my head, I was ready to do some slightly more advanced Mommy Math. Loves to clean? Either she's been pilfering her son's Ritalin or she has a worse relationship with the truth than Dick Cheney. I mentally added a housekeeper two days a week minimum, decided that the word "cleaning" could loosely be translated to getting out of the way to a day spa for a mani/pedi/seaweed wrap so the housekeeper could do her job, and tacked on some round-the-clock day care. I felt so much better I celebrated with a couple more martinis.

Sometimes the only remedy for an overdose of smug is to get yourself in the company of some real moms for a reality check. Real moms will let you in on the fact that they are sometimes inconsistent with their discipline—that they have at times totally lost it over a minor infraction, like their toddler's totally normal refusal to take a bath when asked very nicely and promised "no washing of hair." Real moms will call you in tears because their kid hasn't stopped barfing since she stupidly let him have three huge pieces of cake at a three-year-old's birthday party. Real moms know that trying to limit TV watching to a half hour a day is about as realistic as Kellie Pickler trying to maintain that she didn't get a boob job. Real moms will tell you that their four-and-a-half-year-old is only 80 percent potty trained. Real moms know that when it comes to being a parent, there is no perfect scorecard. No matter how many hours you spend sitting on the floor coloring, reading stories, kissing boo-boos, and singing songs, there will be times you fall short. And most of us just try to accept that as best we can.

But even real moms aren't immune to the urge to keep up with the Smug Mama Joneses. Sometimes you'll find yourself shaving the actual hours you have a sitter to your close friends or feigning surprise that your Little Miss Loves to Read knows all the words to every *Backyardigans* song. It's natural. We live in a competitive world. Like men never lie to other men about their salary, dick size, or lifetime membership to Hair Club for Men?

So okay, fine, my daughter regularly eats cookies, never eats vegetables, and watches two full hours of TV a day. There, I said it. Whatever, go ahead and judge . . . and . . . okay, add two more hours of TV while you're at it.

Mind Your Mommy Manners

Life is different with a toddler tailing you wherever you go. People look at you suspiciously when you walk into a restaurant or even their home. Be mindful of this. Just because we have children, we can't leave broken toys at people's houses and broken spirits of restaurant waiters in our wake.

Who would've thought that people without kids would be put off by your child's beautiful and articulate (and yes, about twenty-five decibels above an adult's comfort level) performance of the *SpongeBob SquarePants* theme song while you're out eating brunch? But they are. And if you're the type of mom who is oblivious to your child's high-pitched screaming and playing Duck, Duck, Goose around the table, just know that it bothers me enough for both of us and I won't be going out to eat with you anymore.

Let's start with the great time killer: taking your kids out to eat. Ever waited tables? I did. In fact, I was a waitress for so many years I'm surprised I have a modicum of self-esteem left. My head still whips around when I hear the word "Miss!" So when I arrive at Chili's with my child, two friends, and their two children, I feel nothing but compassion for the waiter who rolls his eyes a bit when he finds out he's assigned to our table. I wouldn't want to wait on us either.

Too often the kids end up playing drums on the table with the silverware, conducting experiments involving every NutraSweet packet in the restaurant and my Diet Coke, kicking the chairs of innocent diners, and designing spinach dip murals on the booths. Sure, they can't help it, and I have to tolerate a certain amount of toddler behavior if I'm ever going to leave the house, but my waiter shouldn't have to pay the price. That's where becoming a better tipper comes in. Twenty percent is no longer generous; it's the minimum, and 25 percent is better. Is it really going to hurt for everyone to throw in an extra buck? If it is, then next time use the drive-through at McDonald's—just try not to spend an hour and a half at the big Ronald's mouth ordering your Happy Meal, because another mom may be in the car behind you . . . slowly going insane and plotting your demise.

It seems common courtesy sometimes gets thrown out the window when we have children. And at one time or another we're all guilty. Phone etiquette comes to mind. Before I had kids, there was something I found incredibly irritating: people who like to describe what their pet is doing while you're trying to talk to them on the phone. Hey, I don't care how adorable it looks to you, I'm not there! I don't care that Mr. Bojangles just climbed into a drawer all by himself for a catnap. Update me if *Mr. Bojangles* learns to solve a complicated mathematical equation on his paws—just not over the phone.

Now that I have children, people think I want to hear what their baby is doing over the phone. I don't. Again, I can't see it and I have my own child giving me an in-house performance every day. So, unless you're ready to sit through a slide show of my family's last vacation or pore over our Flickr account, keep your narrations to yourself.

Another phone faux pas that I catch myself doing from time to time is interrupting a telephone call with a child-free friend eighteen times to scream to your toddler, "Honey, no. Uh-uh. No! Don't chew on that! Mommy's diaphragm is not a toy. I'm not telling you again! Did you hear me? I said put the diaphragm down! I'm sorry. You were saying that you think you may have a rare blood disorder? Oh, Jesus. Hang on one sec. EMILY, NO! Go on. No not you, Emily. So wait, lupus?" See? That was annoying just reading it, right? Imagine how annoying it is to the person on the other end of the line.

Sometimes we just can't help but have our attention split, especially when we're looking after small children, but that's when you just have to say, "This is a really bad time. Let me call you back the second I put these little monsters to bed." Trust me, you're doing everyone involved a favor. Now if I could just learn to follow my own advice, I might not always reach voice mail when I call my friends. *Damn you*, Caller ID.

Manners need to extend beyond the phone and into personal visits. I'm going to come right out and admit something to you. I'm a flake. It's not a pretty quality, but I've been this way for a long time. Plans for Saturday that sounded somewhat tolerable on Monday have a way of seeming more like Chinese water torture by Friday night. I've been trying to improve this—for about twenty years—but it's slow going. Saying yes to fewer offers helps a little, as does staying away from people who have a need to fill their date books a month in advance, but I'm still a bit unreliable. Even though most moms are fairly understanding, I have learned it's important to at least have a good excuse. I'm certainly not suggesting leaving the house any more often than you have to—come on, it's me you're talking to—I'm simply saying it will serve you to be more inventive.

Unless you're eight months pregnant or ran a marathon earlier that morning, "I'm tired" is a lame excuse for blowing off a playdate. Instead try, "Oh boy, I really want to come over, but I woke up this morning with a weird loose cough." Any mom worth her salt would be willing to pay you to stay away from her children—which can also be a quick way to make an extra twenty bucks.

But have you used the "sick" excuse so many times

that people are beginning to suspect you have TB and friends and neighbors have taken to wearing a surgical mask around you? For a change of pace there's always, "Britney refused to take a nap and she's completely out of control." See? Believable *and* understandable. I can tell you the last thing I'm interested in is having your toddler over to whine and scream and complain about my cooking all afternoon. I have a husband for that. I'm kidding, of course. As if I ever cook.

One rule to remember about flaking: If at all possible, give the recipient of your flakiness at least an hour's warning. There's nothing worse than having someone cancel five minutes before they were supposed to arrive, after you've already wasted three minutes surface cleaning your living room. Clearly it's better to stop flaking than become a compulsive liar, but I'm not a licensed therapist and this isn't a self-help book. Plus, who's got time for self-improvement? I'm way too busy trying to improve other people.

If you fall into the fly-by-night camp like I do, take comfort in the knowledge that some amount of flaking is a given among mothers. Expecting the unexpected is par for the course and is to be tolerated, otherwise you'll finding yourself going through mom friends quicker than *The View* goes through cohosts.

Politeness also counts when you actually get your shit together enough to follow through on plans. When arriving at someone else's house or meeting someone at the mall or other common mommy outings, don't show up empty-handed. If your toddler has a string cheese addiction, don't expect your friend to be your supplier—bring some! A six-pack of Diet Coke or Mike's Hard Lemonade is always a welcome sight as well. If your child is still in diapers, keep in mind that your friend's diaper bag is not a drugstore—come well stocked. That goes double for wipes.

Sometimes you will leave the house and forget everything. Chances are your pal will be happy to hook you up with juice boxes and Pull-Ups, but if you make a habit out of this you will be tagged as a Mommy Mooch and you can expect your invites to dwindle. Take it from someone who knows. Of course, if not getting asked to do stuff is your ultimate goal, then success is a consistently forgotten sippy cup away.

So you're hanging out with a mom friend, and although you forgot a nutritious snack you did find some old raisins in the bottom of your purse and no one's peed on the floor—yet. You're home free, right? Slow down, amigo. There's still the issue of conversation. Other parents are great for relating to your personal parenting woes, but there are limits. Here are just a few conversation killers you may not be aware of.

Complaining: Some people just love to whine. I'm one of them. I've actually been fired from more than one crappy job for my piss-poor attitude, so it takes a lot for me to find someone else's bitching annoying—but it can happen.

I had an acquaintance, *had* being the operative word here, who thrived on bitching about her husband. Each time we got together or spoke on the phone I was greeted with a defeated sigh just before she launched into a blow-by-blow account of their latest spat. "I can't believe him," she'd moan. Her complaints ranged from his not spending enough time with the family to leaving a towel on the bathroom floor to feeding her son french fries to calling her a nagging wench. Granted, her husband was kind of an a-hole, but after listening to her for hours and hours, I kind of saw his point. The only thing I had in common with this woman was having a kid, and now I'm stuck inside her marriage. Listen, we all need to vent sometimes, but if I wanted to be a marriage counselor I would've gone to college. Or at least tried to maintain better than a C average in high school.

Bragging: Bragging is annoying at best and alienating at worst. There is no quicker way to make another mom angry than to be a Bragga-Mama. "I potty trained my daughter in two hours last Saturday afternoon!" Well, guess what, show-off, it smells like she just pooped her pants! "Look! My husband bought me a 1933 gold Patek Philippe watch that was auctioned off at Sotheby's, for no reason!" I can think of a reason, he's cheating on you.

"I just tried on a pair of jeans I've had since junior high school and they still fit!" Let me be the first to congratulate you and then stab you in the eye. Plus, I think we all know that the flip side of bragging is judging, so when this bizzotch isn't busy telling you how great her life is, she's silently condemning yours. Blame it on insecurity if you must, but it's still no fun to be around.

Talking Only About Your Children: I hope, for everyone's sake, that by the time your child has left infancy you've managed to develop a few outside interests. But I've found this isn't always the case. For the first year, talking about your baby's poop consistency and frequency is not only warranted but actually appreciated—especially by other new moms. But after that, most people want to move on to greener pastures and save the tot talk for their pediatrician and partner. There are so many other rich topics for discussion: politics, Paris Hilton . . . okay, maybe there aren't that many, but it's worthwhile trying to force ourselves to come up with some or risk becoming a conversational cipher.

Commenting on Another Mom's Parenting: I don't care if *Parenting* magazine just named you Exemplary Mom of the Year, no one wants to hear a critique on their own parenting style, even if it's in the form of an offhand "Oh, is that all she's having?" Last I checked, it wasn't against the law not to eat broccoli, so until that's officially on the books, I'd appreciate it if you wouldn't cluck disapprovingly at my daughter's dinner of cookies and cheese. And my dinner of vodka and ice.

Talking About Religion: "Ever since I got hooked up to an E-meter, my life has really turned around!" Nothing shuts a conversation down faster than proselytizing. Listen, I'm glad Scientology changed your life, but save the crazy talk for Tom Cruise—I'm not interested. I would imagine at this point in our lives, as far as religion goes, we're all set, so I don't know why certain people find it necessary to try and save my soul. If you insist on quoting the Bible, invoking God's mercy when the kids fight over a toy, or praising Jehovah, I won't be back.

Bringing Up Your Bank Account: If your kid's clothes are designer and you're serving up sashimi for lunch, I can probably guess that you have a lot of money, but we don't need to talk about it. Let's make a deal: If you promise not to bum me out with tales of how sad you are that Mercedes-Benz doesn't make an S-Class in their SUV, I won't bore you with how many great baby clothes bargains I've found on eBay.

Disciplining a Child Who Doesn't Belong to You: Sure I'm going to be seeing red when your kid takes a chomp out of my baby's arm because she dared to touch his Thomas the Train caboose, and no, I probably won't be satisfied by your cooing, "Use your words" when I feel strongly that prying his teeth out with pliers would be much more effective. But doing so would be wrong in the eyes of another parent and the law. If your friend's tyrant is tearing through your house screaming at the top of their little lungs, by all means say, "Hey, spa voices please" in your sternest voice, but spanking, shouting, grabbing, and swearing are currently off-limits.

You have my permission to post these rules on your door if you run into any repeat offenders—similar to the rules you see up at a public swimming pool, they're for your own safety . . . and mine!

Playdates: and Other Potentially Irritating Ways to Spend an Afternoon

One of the more difficult tasks you will face as the mother of a toddler is making friends with other kids' parents. Playdates are a crucial source of midday adult interaction, not to mention someone else's expensive toys for your kid to play with. But finding a civilized tot *and* a fun, simpatico parent can be as tough as hitting the daily double at the track. In arranging a playdate for your toddler, there are so many personality types to match up: Clingy, Independent, Drama queen, the Know-It-All, Bossy, Biter, Waaaay Too Talkative, Won't Share, Picky Eater, Hyperactive, ADD . . . and these are just the parents.

Having someone you genuinely get along with and can just "hang out" with, comparing notes on postbaby sexual activity and bikini waxing while the kids play oh-so-happily, only happens in the best of circumstances or when *Supernanny's* Jo Frost is supervising. But still, to me, it's most important to take pleasure in the other parents' company and share some similar parenting attitudes, because an afternoon with the wrong mom can feel like spending two hours on the Stairmaster with the TV stuck on a *George Lopez Show* marathon. And if you work all day, time is limited, so it's even more important that your playdate partner is at least less boring than your job!

One time-saving trick is to screen out potentially disastrous playdates before they happen. Here is a quiz I give out to prospective moms to see if they are someone whose company I could endure for more than an hour-long stint. You have my permission to copy it and put it to good use. I know, I'm a giver.

1. I show up at your door with a bottle of Pinot Grigio. Your response:
  A) What kind of mother are you?
  B) Oh, I would never drink this early, but I'll store it for you in my two-thousand-dollar Sub-Zero fridge.
  C) Pop that sucker open, bitch.

2. Our children are fighting over a toy. Your response:
  A) Jump up and say, "Sweetie pantsy poo, you *must share*. You have company. It's not nice to take a toy away from someone else. Please give it back and mummy will give you a cookie. OKAY, TWO."
  B) Point out that your child has about a bajillion toys to choose from, and have I thought about buying my child more things to play with?
  C) Unless it leads to fisticuffs, ignore the situation and let them figure it out.

3. I've been at your house for two hours. How many phone calls have you received, answered, and spent an inordinate amount of time talking on?

    A) None. I've been texting the entire time on my BlackBerry. Just business, babe.

    B) Six—"but you must understand, they were all with the pediatrician that I've been paging, because Joshy has a runny nose and I'm getting worried because it's going on day TWO."

    C) I turned my phone off.

4. While at your house we discuss:

    A) How unbelievably quickly your child is catching on to what you and your husband are saying, so you've made a pact to stop swearing, and you have to put a nickel in a jar anytime one of you says "damn" or, God forbid, something worse.

    B) How you've realized that one pair of sweatpants and three embroidered tunic jerseys can be adapted as the perfect wardrobe for any occasion.

    C) Our mutual love of hot salsa, raspberry margaritas, and *Grey's Anatomy*.

5. Your musical taste is:

    A) Well, we mostly listen to Raffi, Barney, and other singers that the kids just *love*. Especially in the car during long drives. Care to come camping with us?

B) Classical, jazz fusion, and of course, lite rock.
   After all, we're over thirty now.

C) Something I've never even heard before, because
   it's only on my new satellite radio—but I love it!

6. Our kids seem a little bored. You whip out:

   A) An interactive educational activity that we can all
      sit on the floor and play together to help enrich
      their minds.

   B) Your best hint that I should leave.

   C) An inflatable pool, two swim diapers, and that
      bottle of chilled wine.

7. The topic of ice cream is broached. Your response:

   A) Oh, Jaden doesn't eat any refined sugar. But there
      are a few natural sorbets that we purchase from a
      health food store bimonthly as a special treat.

   B) We only give treats when Quinton has earned
      them. If he has four gold stars next to his name
      on the chores chart, he is allowed one serving of
      ice cream.

   C) Ice cream? Uh, *yeah*, want some?

8. I tell you I think my eighteen-month-old seems a
little behind with her vocabulary but that the doc says
he's not too concerned. Your response:

   A) I have a speech therapist you should probably

get in touch with immediately. Here, borrow my phone.

B) I'm sure your doctor's right, but my child speaks seven languages already so I can't really relate.

C) Absolutely nothing to worry about. My oldest didn't start speaking until he was fourteen.

9. I jokingly refer to a friend's child who works as a model. Your response:

A) Who's their agent? We're with Elite Little Ladies Modeling School and Agency.

B) Interesting. Do you know a way I could get involved with that? Just look at my kid, she's a natural.

C) What kind of moron would do that to their kid? I will go kill them right now.

I think you know how you did. I don't want to insult you with a scoring system. If you passed, come on over. If not, I'm sure you'll find some friends who are just your speed.

Enjoy these early years when your child will pretty much happily fritter away two hours with any kid whose mom you choose to hang with. These playdates are more for you than them, so take full advantage—because you may not know it at the time, but this is the honeymoon period. You can try out different moms for size and discard them if it's not a good fit easily (the return policy on mom friends is better than Nordstrom's) because your child won't know the difference. They'll only have a distant memory that there were Fruit Roll-Ups involved.

Sooner than we'd like, by the age of maybe two and a half to preschool, your children will start to favor one child over another and whether or not you click with the mother will be a crapshoot.

Mostly, your child's affinity for one child will have to do with other kid's massive toy collections, unlimited access to TV, and abundance of good snacks. This can actually work out well for both you and your shortie, because at this age you will still be accompanying Junior on their outings. If you're stuck with parents who want to get you involved in a rousing game of Capture the Flag with their small charges, limit cookies to half a Fig Newton only after a nutritious snack, and then insist on quiet reading time for the duration of your child's stay, it's probably going to leave both you *and* your child surly. Despite your child's preferences, at this age they can be fairly easily swayed to enjoy their time at another child's house whose mother *you* prefer, with the promise of french fries for dinner. (P.S. This works on me, too.)

Real problems arise when your child hits around four, five, and beyond and decides she is perfectly capable of choosing her own friends, as well as her own paint color for her bedroom walls. FYI, purple is best left for Lakers uniforms and Teletubbies.

Children are young and inexperienced. They are not the best judges of character. Similar to your best single girlfriend who constantly dates psychos, children's antennae are off and they are apt to pick completely inappropriate playmates. Sometimes the draw of these friends is the bad-influence factor: Your little one may be an angel, but under the tutelage of a slightly older, less disciplined kid who thinks a good time is raiding your vibrator drawer, you're in a world of trouble. If the other child's abysmal behavior continues, I feel it's only appropriate to label them a bad seed and cut ties. Sure, the label may stay with them for years to come and they could end up getting shipped off to boarding school, but at least they'll be far away from your kid. It's at this point that no matter how much you like the mom, playdates with their kids may not be in anyone's best interest.

The summer I was sixteen, my younger brother Michael made a new friend in the neighborhood—a little tyrant who is now either incarcerated or working as a highly paid entertainment lawyer. These were the old days—before playdates even had a name—when moms sat around in their living room watching their soaps and sipping sherry, assuming that their sons were in their bedrooms building Legos or playing with plastic army men, not concocting Molotov cocktails out of stuff they pilfered from the garage.

Now to be fair to my brother, he was around eleven, sported some huge, wire-rimmed glasses that took up about three-quarters of his face, was a good candidate for braces, and wasn't exactly turning down friendship offers left and right, so I hardly blame him for spending time with an obvious demon spawn. But the result of their time together turned my sweet, innocent brother into a shoplifter.

One afternoon I received a call from the local CVS, asking me if I was the responsible party for him. I, being the only person home, said yes and walked the mile and a half to the drugstore to bail him out of back-office jail.

It seems Demon Spawn had taught my brother to tamper with the back packaging of G.I. Joes, remove the accessories, pocket them, and replace the package back on the wall. My brother was way too honest to pull off a stunt like this consistently and got himself caught on his very first attempt—yeah, *Ocean's Eleven* it wasn't. When I picked him up, I couldn't help but feel sorry for him, looking so innocent in his navy parka and wool hat with the little pom-pom collapsed forlornly over to one side of his head—and also wonder how he could have failed to notice the *mirrors* on the wall. Come on—that's, like, Shoplifting 101. I took over the role of parent and forbid him to play with Demon Spawn ever again. I figured that evil kid could turn his house into a crack den on his own time without dragging my brother into it.

Basically, unless you want to end up conversing with your child through a plastic screen in juvie, I say do your best to nip these friendships in the bud.

But on the other hand, if your sanity swings in the balance, hang out with the parents you like, even if your child picks up a few bad habits . . . like saying "douchebag" or expecting home-cooked meals.

An alternative to the one-on-one playdate is being part of a larger group of moms who get together with their kids on a fairly regular basis. This is called a playgroup. One thing that's great about this situation is there's safety in numbers, so you can easily forget all about your kid while you scarf down grapes and talk about the great sale at Loehmann's, because there are so many other adults there you can figure *someone's* got to be watching him. Plus, joining a playgroup gives you the chance to hang out with people who under normal circumstances wouldn't be friends with you. One mom I know was lucky enough to find herself in a playgroup where one of the women was married to a professional football player. Not only did my friend get to hang out at their palatial estate, but for her son's birthday party, this woman hired an entire petting zoo to show up! Now there's a big score.

Another advantage to playgroups is that there is usually at least one person in the group far more officious than the rest of you, who will make sure to keep it organized. But be aware: If you allow someone too much authority, your peaceful little democracy may quickly become a dictatorship.

I remember a legendary story of a woman who ran

a playgroup like it was a corporation. Before becoming a mom, she'd run a company with more than sixty employees answering to her—apparently that kind of power is heady stuff, and she was finding it difficult to let go. She attempted to arrange outings with at least thirteen other moms to parks, malls, her house, the zoo, etc. The problem was, as a condition of joining, the other moms were told they had to show up each and every week or risk being kicked out. She actually went as far as to try to have the women sign a document stating their commitment to not miss a week of fun. Obviously, she ended up managing a playgroup for *one* due to her unrealistic expectations—and a few lawsuits over breach of contract. My advice to you if you're ever confronted with paperwork before joining a playgroup is to have a good lawyer look it over. And never hang out with any mom who's more litigious than Michael Jackson.

It's true that thanks to your kids, you will end up spending time with women who will make you wish you were home rearranging your underwear drawer rather than tolerating another twenty minutes of tedious toddler small talk. But keep an open mind. You may find yourself pleasantly surprised that the playdate mom you nearly wrote off due to a WORLD'S GREATEST MOM T-shirt that made you throw up in your mouth a little bit was just being ironic and that, thanks to your kids, that woman ended up becoming one of your closest friends.

Potential Playdate Red Flags

Candy cigarettes rolled up in their sleeves.

Likes the movie *Backdraft* a *little* too much.

Listens to music by the band Anthrax.

Shoots you "the guns" as a greeting.

The other mom lets your son have too many sweets.

Traits You Should Definitely Avoid

An actual Newport dangling from their lips.

Has recently relocated from another state to your
neighborhood under a cloud of suspicion for arson.

Knows of a good website to purchase anthrax.

Knows how to shoot a gun!

The other mom insists that your son call her "sweets."

Part Two:
The Culture of Toddler

Television: It's Not Just for When You're In the Shower!

Since we've cleared up that all kids except those with totally psycho parents are going to be watching TV, and plenty of it, let's just agree that television in moderation isn't fatal. Watching television, even mindless television, does not turn innocent children into serial killers, ne'er-do-wells, or rappers—but it can prevent overworked, on-the-verge-of-hysteria parents from becoming completely unhinged. To me, that's something to be praised, not vilified! Can I get an amen, sister?

Sure, twelve hours of straight viewing is not optimum; television shouldn't be used as a drug (maybe just a mood enhancer), and you don't want your kid watching so much television you are forced to stage an intervention. But TV in moderation (and my moderation may be different from yours) can be a wonderful thing!

Personally, I will go to my grave defending my daughter's viewing habits. After all, her favorite show is *Sesame Street*, which taught us both to count to seventeen; and *Dora the Explorer* has instilled tolerance of other lifestyles.

I mean, come on, are you going to try and convince me that Tico the Squirrel isn't a little light in the loafers? Have you noticed the way he nags Benny the Bull? Have you seen the rainbow sweater? He's either Bill Cosby or a big old queen. You decide. Then there's Dora's best friend, Boots the Monkey, who only needs to *think* about his bright red boots before he starts dancing around like he's at a Ricky Martin concert. I'm just saying . . . every girl needs a gay best friend. Hey, it's no *L Word*, but it is enlightening the tots to some pretty advanced concepts! I love that. And thanks to Dora and Diego, my daughter is officially bilingual, too. I catch her saying Spanish words that I don't even remember from the summer I spent in Spain. Although I don't remember much from my summer in Spain, so that might be a bad example.

I firmly believe that the Spanglish gal with the purple backpack is a positive influence on my child, regardless of whether or not Swiper the Fox glorifies stealing and Dora is turning our kids into full-fledged narcs. I have to admit it's mildly irritating when I attempt to steal a few fries from my kid's Happy Meal and I'm thwarted with a swift and firm, "Swiper, no swiping! Swiper, NO swiping!"

My only issue with my toddler's Dora obsession is the nails-on-chalkboard theme song. I defy you to get *"Doo doo doo doo DORA! Dora Dora Dora the Explorer"* out of your head for more than twenty seconds a day. But even that's a small price to pay for my daughter's new language skills; she's outside negotiating with our gardener for a good price on tree trimming right now! Bonus!

While most babies will be equally enthralled by Baby Einstein videos, *So You Think You Can Dance?* or a fly walking across the screen, toddlers tend to have a more discerning viewing palate. Gone are the days where you could breast-feed to your heart's content while deeply engrossed in *ER*. Now your child will have his/her very own favorite shows and will insist that if the television is on, it *will* be tuned to one of these programs. Seeing as you will spend the bulk of your child's allotted TV time doing other more important things . . . like reading the Internet, I do recommend at least being semiconscious of what they're watching.

Years ago the worst thing that could invade your living room was a big purple dinosaur. Now we've got a slew of potentially offensive viewing options. Take those slutty Bratz; do you really want your child emulating a cartoon character who dresses like a walking AMBER Alert? The Bratz consist of six scantily clad, self-proclaimed fashionistas with deep philosophical interests, like "blueberry pancakes." If your child insists on watching them, do yourself a favor and go to their official website, where you can check out all the kewl merchandise. The Bratz Big Babyz doll is decked out in skintight boy shorts and a belly shirt. Yeah, that's an appropriate outfit for a one-year-old. An eighteen-month-old in a micromini and teeny tank makes perfect sense—but a one-year-old? That's pushing it. I got so mad watching this show that I threw the remote control right through the screen of the seven-thousand-dollar plasma TV—which was a huge problem, mainly because I wasn't at my house.

As parents, it's our responsibility to know what our kids are watching and which shows may have adverse affects on our children's still forming brains. So to help you out and save you a little time, I've compiled a list of must-avoids!

Wonder Pets—And in the category of Theme Song Most Likely to Drive a Pregnant Woman to Drink, the Academy award goes to *Wonder Pets!* Oh, if only it were just that the theme song is annoying. The show centers around three friends with major issues who have deluded themselves into thinking that the world's problems can be solved through teamwork—pretty naive, fellas. First there's Linny, the bulimic guinea pig, who blurts out, "This calls for some celery!" no matter how inappropriate the occasion. Then there's Turtle Tuck, a needy little guy who's constantly asking for hugs from any random stranger who will oblige him—abandonment issues, anyone? And finally, rounding out the dysfunctional trio is Ming-Ming Duckling, who, despite the disclaimer at the start of each episode that the show is designed to build vocabulary in preschoolers, has an obvious speech impediment. You need to hear her catchphrase "this is sewious" just the once to want to deep-fry her ass.

Doodlebops—If you want your child exposed to their first ménage à trois, this is the show for you. Three very jauntily dressed musicians (one female, two male) hang out, play games, and wear a lot of makeup. There's Rooney, the grossly effeminate guitarist; Deedee, the raunchy little go-go girl with the big voice; and Moe, the "cool" drummer who is always hiding in the Doodlebops Central "closet." The supporting cast includes Jazz and Bus Driver Bob, two alternates in the ongoing tryst among the main characters. Sure the sexual messages may be subliminal, but if you freeze-frame the episode where Deedee gets her dancing shoes, you'll see what looks a little too much like a bondage mask fall out of the prank closet. And I swear Rooney and Moe once made a rhyme about the time they "crossed swords." Kids may find it endlessly entertaining, but I'm sorry, it's just too high a price to pay for thirty minutes of peace and quiet.

The Wiggles—You'll know you've been home with the kids too long when you start having sexual fantasies about Anthony, the cutest Wiggle, and by far the most charismatic. But he will frequently dash your hopes when he trots out his lovely Italian wife and his kids. Please tell me he doesn't love her! Who needs that kind of disappointment in an already trying day? Plus, the other characters aren't exactly setting a good example for the kids: Jeff, I think, has a developmental delay. He is always just a little off rhythmically. Captain Feathersword just sounds like a failed porn star. He's most likely still using the name because it's already monogrammed onto his regular clothes, or initialed onto the side of his Camaro.

Blue's Clues—Luckily for me, my daughter doesn't seem to like this half-hour borefest any more than I do. The trouble with this show is all the drama surrounding the original host, Steve Burns. First there were a slew of rumors that the guy died of a heroin overdose, which turned out to false—although if they were true, who could've blamed him, really? If I was forced to wear a green striped rugby shirt and beige chinos every day of my life, I'd be snorting a little shmackedy-shmack myself. Then later he pulls a David Caruso and leaves the show at the height of its popularity to pursue his dream of playing in a nameless rock band. Now the only publicity this guy's getting is through his MySpace page. Good thinking, Steve! Looks like we figured out who really needs to get a clue. But when Joe, Steve's replacement, appears in random episodes, and your innocent baby asks, "Mama, where's Steve?" *you* try explaining all the sordid details without causing nightmares. Confusing and disturbing.

Dragon Tales—So there you are minding your own business, eating a piece of toast with peanut butter on it and checking your e-mails while your little sweetie kicks back for the PBS Kids morning lineup, when suddenly you sense something's wrong. You come out of your office to find your heretofore engaged toddler scraping a quarter along your coffee table, leaving welts as deep as tire tracks while simultaneously using your cell phone to call Japan. What went so terribly wrong? You glance up at the television only to see a two-headed dragon named Zak and Wheezie (and no, not the Weezy from *The Jeffersons*). *Dragon Tales* is what went wrong. *Dragon Tales* is the wrench thrown right between *Clifford* and *It's a Big Big World*. It mainly involves Max and Emmy, the most earnest kids on the planet, and not a half a personality between them. Every episode, these two go off to Dragon Land to have fun and adventures *plus* learn a lesson, which would be well and good if it held a child's attention longer than an NPR radio show. A program that can't keep your toddler occupied gets rated a D for downright dangerous.

Thomas & Friends—Here's the rundown of this British snoozer. Thomas the Train (wreck) and a bunch of other tank engines with stuffy names like Percy, James, Edward, Gordon . . . I'm sorry, I drifted off for a minute while I was typing this . . . live on the fictional island of Sodor. If your child was literally born yesterday they might not notice how old-school this is, but the real problem for me lies with the upper-crust British narration. Do you really want your toddler imitating this speech pattern? It can only lead to schoolyard beatings for walking around with a pathetic fake British accent. Just look at Madonna.

Nip/Tuck—At first glance this doesn't even seem like a kids' show at all. Call me old-fashioned, but I'm not sure gory boob jobs and tummy tucks are appropriate subjects for babies. But even more disturbing, the plot lines are not challenging enough for even the youngest of viewers. My daughter was completely over it by season two.

On the flip side, there are plenty of shows that don't make me want to poke myself with a shish kebab skewer. The Alterna-dads and -moms may disagree, but I find *Jack's Big Music Show*, *Arthur*, *Clifford the Big Red Dog*, and *Dora* and *Diego* to be appointment television. *Backyardigans?* Bring 'em on. I have nothing but love for this clearly integrated group of animated singing creatures with names like Uniqua, Pablo, and Tyrone—they sing, they dance, and they all share one backyard, just like on *Big Love!* Furthermore, I'd watch *Sesame Street* or any vintage *Sesame Street* DVD or music special *on my own*, and not just to be ironic. But if you are going to actually sit down and watch TV with your little one, be prepared. There are very few forensic psychologists, elimination rounds, or surprising home renovations to be found in children's programming, and it can get tedious, so you may want to bring a magazine. But hey, it's called being a parent. So do it. You can always TiVo *Survivor: Bakersfield*.

All this being said, how can you tell if the amount

of TV they watch is too much? Here are a few warning signs your kid *may* be spending too much time in front of the boob tube.

He refers to his dad (who, granted, works a lot of hours) as "a character on that one show."

She has a favorite cleaning product commercial.

At two, her vocabulary is limited to *Wonder Pets* catch-phrases.

She watches more TV than you do.

Your daughter tells you her dream is to have a pony—a "My Little Pony."

When the TV is off, he worries it's broken.

I Don't Like You—I Don't Like You, Either

There are going to be days upon days when you can't believe how much you love your toddler. It's a giddy new romantic love, a blinding love where they can absolutely do no wrong. One day you'll be looking at them over your morning coffee while they contentedly watch *Sesame Street*, assessing the intricacies of Ernie and Bert's latest spat like it's the Middle East conflict, and you won't know whether to smother them with wet kisses or help them apply for early admittance to Princeton.

Like in the early days of dating my husband, when it was awe-inspiring just to watch him sleep, I often stand over my daughter while she naps, memorizing the way she looks with her blanket wrapped around her head turban-style like a tiny 7-Eleven cashier, the spent sippy cup she still clutches in her hand, and the two huge books threatening to make a permanent indentation on her cheek because she insisted on taking them to bed. I can't get enough of her laugh, especially when I threaten (and it's no empty threat) to eat her tummy for lunch. I can't get enough of her smiles, her curiosity, her constant question "Wassthis?" to any object for which she doesn't know the name. I love that she makes me drive her all around the neighborhood to look for Christmas lights in the middle of summer. I love being her mother, the person who will shape the way she knows love forever. I love my child.

But there are those occasions when I don't like her. At all. Case in point: My husband and I were flying home from Connecticut one Christmas, where we had just paid a visit to his parents. Taking a child out of state is hard enough, but for a full ten days we were dealing with a borrowed Pack 'N Play as a crib. In spite of my sister-in-law's assurances, counting on a glorified playpen to contain a thirty-pound two-year-old bent on escape is like trying to keep David Blaine in chains underwater: It's both impossible and *really* annoying. Our detainee broke out of her makeshift cell every single night and stumbled around in the dark, breaking small expensive figurines like a drunk lady browsing at Tiffany. By seven a.m. she'd finally drift off to sleep, leaving us a full ninety minutes of shut-eye to start the day.

Add to this stress cocktail my suspicion that my father-in-law thinks I'm an emotional, outspoken alien sent from out of space to torture him with inappropriate household behavior, like not wearing shoes to the dinner table. But I managed to survive it all with the time-honored trio of sulking, drinking to excess, and daily Holly Hunter-esque crying spells.

When we got to the airport for our flight home, I assumed all the stress was now past: Just a few sleepy hours on the red-eye, punctuated by a quick landing in Dallas for a yummy snack and a diaper change, and we'd be as good as back in our own bed. It didn't work out that way. Ned Beatty had a smoother time canoeing down backwoods rivers than we had getting back home.

Looking back, the seeds had been sown long before we departed. My darling daughter woke up that morning at four a.m. Why? Because it seemed like the perfect wake-up time for the day we were *flying home* twelve hours later. Naturally, she refused a nap, and we found ourselves boarding the first leg of our American Airlines flight with an extremely overtired carry-on toddler. Luckily, she behaved like a normal child on the first leg, even dozing a bit as expected. But by the time we trudged through the airport and changed planes in Dallas, she had worked herself into a state seen only in movies starring Linda Blair. From the moment we boarded the plane, she cried and didn't stop. I am not exaggerating when I tell you that she yelled and screamed and tantrumed for *hours*. My blood pressure is dangerously high just typing this. I'd never heard of a child being able to keep up a crying fit for that long. And it was so unlike my daughter that I was at a loss on how to deal with the situation.

I tried everything: three mini bottles of red wine, earplugs, watching Robin Williams in *RV* . . . I also did everything I could think of to comfort her. At the offers of cuddling, stories, DVDs, snacks, or drinks, she writhed in agony, threw sippy cups at passengers' heads, and swatted my much-needed wine into my lap. Out of desperation, I even let her pick a corn dog fryer out of *SkyMall* magazine, 'cause it stopped the tears for all of two seconds before they resumed in earnest. No, Dr. McScreamy wasn't going down without a fight.

The flight attendants tried everything too. Well, not everything. I later heard about a male flight attendant who was arrested and subsequently fired from an airline for slipping a toddler, who'd been screaming for hours, some crushed-up Xanax in its juice. Isn't that the worst thing you ever heard? Fired? I mean, a person goes above and beyond to give good service and that's the thanks they get? No one offered up any drugs on my flight—just bad suggestions.

"Maybe she's teething," came from the seat behind us.

"She's done teething. She's two and a half. She's just really tired."

"They can still be teething at two and a half." I seriously wished there was seating on the wing.

"Maybe she needs to go to sleep," came one genius hint from across the aisle. Ya think?

This is when I took my cue and started walking her up and down the length of the plane. I felt like the worst mother in the world—on parade! And by the stares we were getting, it was like I was wearing a sign that said THIS MOTHER CANNOT COMFORT HER POOR, OBVIOUSLY-IN-PAIN OR

SEVERELY TRAUMATIZED DAUGHTER. I made sure to bring her into first class just to make sure they don't forget how the other half kicks it back in coach.

I know she was beyond tired, and I'm assuming her ears hurt, because I'd like to give her an excuse for behaving like a faulty smoke detector, but the stress, embarrassment, and my own lack of sleep were eating away at my compassion. My daughter and I had entered into enemy camps. I actually felt mad, furious even. And hopeless. At one point I completely gave up and read *People* magazine while she wailed. But ignoring her didn't work like it does on my husband.

The devil child continued to yell relentlessly until about thirty minutes before we landed, which happened to be the stroke of midnight on December 31. That's how my husband and I brought in 2007. Happy fucking New Year.

In the days that followed, my daughter and I needed to re-bond. In my opinion, we needed some time apart, but she, being the more mature one, felt we could talk it out. In all honesty, I felt disconnected from her, and more than that, guilty for feeling anything but undying love. I wondered if there was something wrong with me. After telling my therapist, my friends, and a woman I met at Kinko's how bad I felt about those days of disliking my own baby, they reassured me that this was perfectly normal and happens to the best of us. Eventually we both got back to our old selves, and I resumed tummy eating in earnest.

But, trust me, it's happened again and again; never as bad as the plane fiasco (so far). But there are days the only word out of her mouth all day is "NO." And there are times she has tantrums for no reason in the middle of a bookstore or pharmacy and I secretly wish that she'd stub her toe or that Nickelodeon would cancel *Dora*.

Here's the bottom line. If you resent your toddler because he prevents you from going to happy hour at Moose McGillycuddy's three nights a week, I really can't help you. But if you find that some days you just want to pawn your three-year-old off on a kindly retired neighbor and pick up your child-free existence where you left off, you're not alone. Try to remember, when you are in the throes of a bad day, week, year: Treat it like turbulence; hang on tight, breathe deeply, and drink 'em if you got 'em. You will land eventually, and you will be happy again. I was. That is, until UPS dropped off my SkyMall corn dog fryer along with a bill for $69.99.

The Littlest Dictator: How I Deal with Tantrums and Screaming with Only a Minimum of Nonprescription Drugs

Even though it's possibly the most difficult part of parenting, we've all witnessed enough bad-behaving starlets to know that kids need limits and boundaries. And as much as it pains you, in order to show your child where the line is, and not raise a future Lindsay Lohan, sometimes you will have to brave being the heavy.

The first time I gave my daughter a real live time-out, the kind where it's actually punitive and not just a way to let the kid cry themselves calm, I felt like I'd morphed into Mommy Dearest. She was ranting and raving way too early one morning because I committed the cardinal sin of starting the coffeemaker without giving her ample opportunity to push the button. Actually, as per our tradition, I'd asked her if she would *like* to push the button, but it seemed she and Elmo were having a private moment and I was intruding with my rude question, and I got a curt "No." But a minute later, when her bionic hearing picked up the sound of coffee brewing, she went completely mental. "You pushed the button! I wanted to push it! MAMA! PLEASE! I need to push the button!" she screamed as if I wasn't in the same room with her or even the same county.

When I asked her to please give the histrionics a rest, she looked me straight in the eye, balled up her fists, and shrieked louder. She knew exactly what she was doing— and what she was doing was damaging my hearing worse than the time I made the horrible mistake of attending Ozzfest.

I told her in no uncertain terms that if she wanted to continue screaming, she would have to go to her room. I was fairly certain that she knew I meant business, because I channeled my best Cesar Millan the Dog Whisperer voice. She chose to continue screaming defiantly, which meant at this point I'd have to follow through or else be guilty of giving her mixed messages.

"You are getting a time-out," I said, sounding less and less familiar to myself. Taking her by the arm, I attempted to guide her toward her bedroom, and I think she was so startled she momentarily forgot to scream or struggle and let me lead her quietly down the hall. Wow, this was much simpler than I thought! I only wished someone was catching my disciplinary prowess on video! Right then and there I decided to host my own version of *Nanny 911*—but before I could even call my agent, the shock wore off and my daughter's screaming resumed, only quite a few decibels louder. I got her to her bedroom and plopped her onto her bed, but she violently squirmed out of my grasp and leaped off like a dog desperately trying to escape from Animal Control. I firmly put her right back in. She instantly got back out, crying hot, wet tears of anguish and betrayal. I put her back in. She got back out.

"Mama, please stop! Please, please no. I don't wanna stay in my bed!" The look on her face was absolutely heartbreaking. Despite the pain in my chest and my certainty that this would end up in the movie version of her life, I calmly and wordlessly put her back in, where she actually stayed for the requisite two minutes, which seemed more like two hours. But I did it. And even though I cried afterward, she miraculously stopped! It worked— although I didn't forget to let her man Mr. Coffee anytime soon.

Just know that once you get the time-out thing down, don't be surprised when your child tries to give *you* a time-out. "Go to your room and take a nap, Mama," my daughter once commanded when I had the audacity to tell her five cookies was enough. I had to stifle a laugh, mainly because I would have sold my house for a nap.

When it comes to any type of discipline, consistency is definitely something to strive for, but we all know it's a lofty goal. For me, hitting is a behavior that warrants immediate action right then and there, yet when it comes to whining, sometimes it's easier to just pop a Tylenol and tolerate it for a while than to engage in a constant battle of wills. Isn't that why God invented Prozac? I know, I know, some "experts" may say "Whoa, whoa, consistency is *key*, and if you give a child an inch they'll be running your life in no time." True to a point, but you don't have to be a consistency fanatic. These experts are not living in your house with your toddler. In fact, many so-called experts are not living with a kid at all!

I say, if you want to maintain your sanity, pick your battles. If your child wakes up at the earlier-than-usual hour for him and unspeakably horrific hour for you of five forty-five a.m., insisting that they watch "just one episode of *Diego*," part of you may be thinking, *Hey, if I give in now, it may come back to bite me in the ass.* But be reasonable with yourself and your child. You need to weigh how badly you'd like an extra half hour of shut-eye against the low probability that this exception to the rule will create a monster who pops out of bed wide-eyed at five forty-five a.m. jonesing for their Diego fix *every single day from now on.* But please don't hold me to this. Just to be safe, I have an unlisted number.

The sad fact is, even if you're as consistent as Mary freakin' Poppins, all the time-outs in the world won't stop your child from being a moody, irrational tyrant one day and more charming than Patrick Dempsey the next.

It may just be the simple fact that toddlers come with their own personalities and opinions. They have definite attitudes about how their day should unfold, which rarely jibe with yours. This will inevitably lead to power struggles. You thought it was hard getting your husband to go see the latest Hugh Grant movie with you—try convincing your kid to go with you to the bank or at least to behave while you conduct a simple, two-minute ATM transaction. Unless there are balloons or toys, it just ain't going down without a fight.

As inconvenient as it may be, no longer can you just stick them in the BabyBjörn and hit the grocery store or Indian casino. Now you have to consider their interests, and nine times out of ten their interests involve buying toys, eating Gummi Worms, and discussing lions. If they filled out a profile on eHarmony.com, you'd never be a match. And if you were accidentally sent on a blind date, chances are you wouldn't be able to agree on a restaurant, let alone make it through the chicken fingers before you said, "Check, please." But unlike a blind date, you can't get a friend to call your cell phone and pretend there's a family emergency or just do tequila shots to get through it. You're pretty much stuck with your impulse-control-challenged new partner. The sooner you realize your toddler is not purposely trying to drive you crazy, they're just being their own person, the happier you'll be.

Kids are going to act out when they're tired, bored, or for no reason at all. They're wired like that. It's normal and usually not a reflection of bad parenting. Trust me, I've asked around. Sometimes I'll ask my daughter what she wants for dinner while she's watching a video, and she'll refuse to acknowledge that any sound left my mouth. And I know I'm not the only one whose child

says, "No talking!" when I'm trying to have a simple conversation with my husband that, God forbid, doesn't
include her. I have to catch myself, now and then, doing
what she says until I remember, hey, she doesn't sign my
paychecks! I'll talk if I want to!

Of course, some of your child's bad behavior may go
beyond the run-of-the-mill mood swings. But before you
buy out the discipline section of your local bookstore or
hire a live-in child psychologist, you may want to check
the source. Kids are like tiny sea sponges soaking up all
the nutrients and all the garbage floating by them in the
ocean of life. Has two-and-a-half-year-old Olivia mysteriously started calling you an "asswipe" when you try
to strap her into her car seat? Before washing her mouth
out with antibacterial soap, you may want to ask yourself
where she might have heard that word—could it have
been from you? No? Are you sure? What about last week
when some *asswipe* cut you off in traffic, and when you
drove by the cocksucker to flip him off you realized he
was on his goddamned phone? Mystery solved.

I have a friend whose toddler daughter went through
a phase where she consistently barked out commands at
her like some kind of mini drill sergeant. Discipline was
having no effect on her normally sweet-natured girl until
she, too, checked the source. All through my friend's
second pregnancy, she realized she'd been hypercritical
of her husband and that her daughter's tone was only
reflecting back her own bitchy demeanor of the last nine

months. Changing the way she spoke to her husband worked miracles on her daughter and marriage.

Demanding, unreasonable toddlers could also be suffering from the too-much-power syndrome. Too much power was not attractive on Mussolini, and it's even less attractive on your average toddler. Ever been around a parent who starts off every sentence about their two-year-old by whining, "He won't let me"—as in *He won't let me put him down, cut his fingernails, mix a martini*, etc.? Um, last time I checked, you outweighed him by at least a hundred pounds. Man up.

I made the mistake of inviting to my baby shower a "he won't let me" woman with a bossy four-year-old who *always* got his way. The little shit ran around ripping open all my presents. By the time I waddled over to assess the damage, there was an enormous pile of wrapping paper, bows, and decorative rattles lying there, and *he* was crying. Apparently he hadn't registered for a Medela hospital-grade breast pump and wanted to return it for some Power Rangers. I looked to his mom to take control, but she just gave me a "what am I gonna do?" shrug, dipped a baby carrot into some ranch dressing, and had the nerve to ask for another mimosa. I was appalled, but it was clear that the mom knew who ran the kingdom now and she had no intention of taking back the reins. Knowing this was a lost cause, I said nothing, but I never invited them over again. And I never got her the damn mimosa!

Sometimes your child's acting out is just a phase

caused by a stressful transition in their life. Did you move? Go back to work? Add a new baby to the family? Get a new, too-short summer haircut? Did your toddler start preschool? Did you add a new baby to the family? Count on quite a few months of disturbing new habits: Biting, crying, yelling, refusing to sleep . . . ever, wanting constant attention, and even trying to hurt a new baby can be expected. I know that new behavior can be scary, and tough to deal with, especially if you've just had another baby. It may seem like your toddler is prepping for a lifelong career as a prolific serial killer, but I promise, if you don't overreact, your toddler will eventually return to their previous only slightly demonic self. On the other hand, kids who scream, hit, bite, consistently talk back, steal, break things on purpose, or otherwise make your life miserable for no discernable reason may be missing something vital in their life: the word NO. Look into it.

Baby Bling Bling

Remember when you were little and thought an empty Pez dispenser plus a handful of paper clips equaled a full day of fun? And finding a ginormous refrigerator box was cause for celebration for you and every kid in your neighborhood? Or how about when you could burn off an afternoon proving to your friends that you could eat an entire lemon without grimacing? Okay, maybe that last one was just me, but in any case, no matter what you played with as a kid, times have changed, attention spans have dwindled, and the price of entertaining your kids has gone way up.

Toys are going to be (if they aren't already) your child's biggest obsession in life—much the way empty calories are in mine—and I wouldn't bother fighting this if I were you. You may ask yourself why your toddler needs so many toys; why every time you pass any trinket made with brightly colored plastic, your little one suddenly *has to have it* and will throw a monumental meltdown to illustrate to you just how necessary this thing is to their very existence. Question it all you like, but the fact is, there's no valid explanation. Just like there is no way for me to explain why I come home with yet another pair of black chunky shoes—so perfect, so *me*. "And so exactly like every pair you already own," my husband will, oh so unhelpfully, try to reason. How do I explain the subtle difference, which is not visible to the naked eye, to someone who sees no problem with wearing cargo pants to a black-tie-optional dinner? I can't. There is no reasoning with shoes, just as there is no reasoning with toys. The sooner you accept this, the sooner you can stave off bankruptcy and still keep up with your child's toy habit.

There are as many types of toys as there are shoes, and if your little shopper is anything like me, they will want to own many "pairs" from every category. But be warned: It's a short leap from a healthy preoccupation to a full-blown compulsion.

Here's a handy rundown of the basic toy groups you will find yourself up against:

Stuffed Animals—Most toddlers get the whole social life ball rolling by having relationships with their stuffed animals. It's not unusual for your two- or three-year-old to have upwards of thirty "friends," who all have names, must sleep in their crib or bed, and have to accompany your toddler to birthday parties and preschool interviews. The question is: Where do they come from? I don't believe I've personally bought a single stuffed pal for my daughter, yet somehow they multiply like gremlins. I'm pretty sure I caught one rifling through my wallet the other night—but I had consumed a few glasses of wine, so I didn't tell anyone about the incident. The only way I've found to keep the stuffed animal population under control is to systematically remove a bear or two who's not in the inner circle and relocate them to the garage. Don't toss them out, though—trust me, sooner or later your toddler will start screaming that someone kidnapped "Bentley," and there won't be a good night's sleep for the next six years.

Theme Toys—Dora and Diego, Hello Kitty, Bob the Builder, anything with a damn princess on it . . . the list goes on and on. This type of toy is one of the worst budget sucks you can imagine, because no matter how many you buy, every day fifty new ones—better ones—take their place. Take My Little Pony: These people at Hasbro are evil geniuses. They're constantly churning out new horses that are *exactly* the same but with a different name and slightly different hue of pink. I should know—my daughter owns at least thirty and still wants more. But I have to draw the line at purchasing anything from the Disney Store. I'm sorry, but Walt's estate has enough dough—he doesn't need $29.99 of my hard-earned money for a Cinderella pencil sharpener.

Dress-Up—I don't know what it is, but kids love a costume. The calendar doesn't have to say it's anywhere in the vicinity of Halloween for your child to want to go to Wal-Mart decked out in full Spider-Man regalia. If you don't keep kid-friendly tiaras, magic wands, and capes around the house, your children will resort to rummaging through your closet, and you will end up escorting a three-year-old boy out on the town decked out in your Jimmy Choo heels and carrying your Kate Spade handbag. Not that there's anything wrong with it . . .

Making a Mess—Magic markers, stamps with "washable" ink, finger paints, glitter, slightly melted crayons, and Elmer's glue are just a few toys destined to destroy any surface in your house with the balls to be a light color. In fact, there are about as many of these toys as there are cleaning products incapable of washing them out. You may think those pens that draw only on special paper are the answer to your prayers, but unfortunately, they have a weird two-second lag time from when you put pen to paper—irritating to most toddlers, whose attention span is only *one* second. Plus, leave the cap off for ten minutes and they're toast. Best just cover all your furniture with plastic and hope for the best. It worked for my grandmother.

The Toy Inside the Happy Meal—Also included in this category: The "surprise" found in a sugary breakfast cereal box, items your child "accidentally" takes home from the toy aisle in the grocery store, toys from the 99 cents store, and that old gross infant squeaky toy covered in dog spit your kid found at the park. The thing about the toys that cost less than a dollar is that they ironically hold your child's interest for *way* longer than the forty-five-dollar Melissa & Doug wooden musical instrument collection that my daughter *had* to have. But I'm not bitter.

Toys with Lots of Small Parts—I don't know how it happened, but my living room is littered with dollhouse paraphernalia: teacups no bigger than my pinkie nail, miniature chair cushions, and teeny slip-on shoes, not to mention all the tiny plastic marker caps and the *A* key from my computer. Yes, my house has turned into a living, breathing choking hazard for pets and small children. It just seems like so many toys that are attractive to youngsters have a lot of little parts. I don't know what you can possibly do about it, short of putting orange cones all over the place to indicate a danger zone, or . . . vacuuming. But that seems a bit extreme.

Educational Toys—When I say educational, I'm not talking about glow-in-the-dark stars or a bald eagle finger puppet—no, those are fun. I'm talking about items that are designed strictly to improve a child's intellect, like flashcards, encyclopedias, or an abacus. You'll recognize the "toys" in your house that fall in this irksome group by their pristine, never-been-played-with condition. Usually given to your child by distant relatives, judgmental other moms, and ex-teachers, these toys should be appropriately oohed and aahed over and then promptly regifted.

Toys That Make Noise—By far the worst offender in all toy categories, these are items that talk, play music, have sound effects, or God forbid, do all three. Naturally, toddlers and noisy toys go together like cops and mustaches, so somehow you will end up acquiring more than a normal adult can tolerate. Nothing makes my toddler happier than playing a fake plastic guitar that blasts loud, barely intelligible, prerecorded riffs with a push of a button where the strings should be. I have my doubts that Slash learned this way, but for some reason my daughter owns two of them. One major warning: These headache inducers are often possessed and have a tendency to go off spontaneously at four in the morning, leading you to believe your house is haunted, which may prompt you to immediately attempt to sell for ten thousand dollars less than its market value. The only defense against these toys is to conveniently run out of batteries—permanently—*or* have your eardrums surgically removed.

You've scanned your house and realized your child has an inordinate amount of toys. Now it's honesty time;

you need to assess whether or not your child simply has a problem or has become a full-blown toyaholic. The results of toy addiction can be devastating to victims and their families. Ever see a kid in a manic state throwing himself on the floor in the middle of Toys "R" Us because his mom won't buy him yet another Elmo figurine? This little boy was once living a normal, productive life until his addiction took over. Now he's living with a monkey on his back—and it ain't Curious George.

Take this quiz to see if your child's innocent love of toys has turned into a full-blown addiction. Caught early enough, most toddlers can still be helped.

1. Has your child ever been on a toy-playing binge and had no recollection of it the next day?

2. Has your child ever missed a year of preschool because he was too busy playing with toys?

3. Does your child refer to the toy department in Target as her *real* home?

4. Do you find yourself buying toys just to keep the peace?

5. Have you been forced to take a second mortgage on your house to keep up with your child's toy habit?

6. Does your child subject himself or herself to biters, poopers, or other troubled playmates strictly because they have a superior toy collection?

7. Does your child play with toys first thing in the morning even if she already played with them the night before?

8. Does your child play with toys "alone"?

9. Are you afraid to come home from work without a toy?

10. Does your child break into a sweat at the mere sight of Geoffrey the Giraffe and the Toys "R" Us logo?

Don't ignore the warning signs. Sure, a toyaholic toddler may be harmless now, but left untreated, these children grow up to be toyaholic adults. Your three-year-old Game Boy abuser may turn into a thirty-five-year-old action-figure collector who spends all his money at Japanese anime expos, leaving you with a dwindling chance you'll ever see grandchildren. Don't be in denial! Just remember, toddlers have no money, and a two-year-old is slightly too young for an allowance, so it will be up to you to decide when or *if* they get the myriad of items their little hearts desire. But don't be too hard on yourself; sometimes the best you can do when faced with a toy-buying situation is to try and steer your child toward something less expensive. And right after that, try to get Lil' Kim to move away from diamonds and over to some cubic zirconia.

Sickos

If it seems like your toddler is always sick, it's because they are. From the common cold to a scary bout of dehydration that can land your child in the pediatric intensive care unit faster than you can down a bowl of Cherry Garcia, stressful situations with your toddler's health can be a constant. Life with a child is chock-full of the horrors of sniffles, rectal thermometers, and lazy ER doctors. Not to mention the daily bumps and scrapes that are sure to get you sideways looks from the childless. We all know that look, and we all understand why we get it. Most toddlers walk around looking like a battered wife, with ugly bruises on their face and blood splotches in their hair (which haven't been washed out because they act like having their hair washed is against the Geneva Convention). So, yeah, people who have nothing better to do than judge your parenting may give you a concerned look.

But never fear, even if this childless busybody calls the authorities, Social Services is way too understaffed to deal with the many complaints they get to notice your kid, who fell off the monkey bars for the seventh straight day.

You may falsely blame yourself for the daily accidents involving plastic butter knives, a pair of needle-nose pliers left carelessly on the washing machine, a rusty thumbtack innocently dropped deep in a shag carpet that only a psychic or a nosy toddler could find, a cup of scalding McDonald's coffee you meant to put out of reach but somehow found its way to the edge of your desk. But realistically, your kid could get a concussion from a cotton ball. They're built like that. They will find a way to injure themselves. I like to chalk it up to creativity and think of my constantly bruised child as gifted.

Luckily for us, some genius invented Band-Aids with pictures of Batman, princesses, and Dora on them. Children believe in the magic of a Band-Aid's healing power like adults believe in *The Secret*. They are sadly misled but feel better just the same.

Unfortunately, no one can prepare you for when your child really is sick. Injury is one thing. At least you know the source and can take the appropriate action. But sickness is a different animal. It may creep up on you, teasing you with a mild fever, endless whining, a runny nose, and a sudden disinterest in touching things she's forbidden to touch, and slowly become a full-fledged scare. Or it may come on like driving into a brick wall.

One night you put your sweet-smelling child to bed and wake up to the same child covered in vomit, running a fever of 109 degrees, and sweating like a pro wrestler.

I have been through this and (luckily) back, a couple of times in my daughter's short years—and it's not because she was breastfed for only four weeks, so please, no letters about the benefits of breast-feeding and how it can stave off everything from tetanus to tennis elbow. I get it. But just know that kids sometimes get sick out of nowhere, most often the day you're scheduled to leave for an expensive prepaid European vacation or in the middle of your big work presentation.

The first time I had to rush my daughter to the ER, she was only a year old, and wouldn't you know it, my husband had just left the night before on a trip. This is a Murphy's Law of baby sickness: Husbands rarely get puked on because they seem to have a sixth sense about when the kid is going to be ill and hightail it out of town on a "business trip." Although strangely, they lack that same sixth sense that you could use some help with the endless laundry . . . but I digress. My baby woke up in her crib covered in puke around six a.m. Other than needing a bath, she seemed fine, although she refused to eat or drink all day. And yes, I tried everything: popsicles, Pedialyte, peppermint schnapps . . . you name it, she swatted it away like it was Windex. Around midnight her fever spiked to 103 and she started puking more than me the day after my senior prom; so in a slight panic, I loaded her up and headed for the hospital.

You must brace yourself for your first ER experience. The majority of people who work in ERs look nothing like George Clooney and would make Dr.

House seem like a contender for Mr. Congeniality. I've never met anyone doing intake who didn't have the personality of an off-duty meter maid. No matter how small or sick the infant in your arms is, you will be met with a curt "fill out the paperwork, bitch." Okay, the "bitch" will be implied.

I personally waited for hours to see a doctor on my first trip, and I use the term "doctor" loosely because (a) I'd been waiting for five hours, so I was a tad irritable and (b) the "doctor" actually said, "Maybe she's just colicky." *Maybe she's just colicky? Are you high?* Which immediately reminded me of that old joke: What do you call a person who graduated last in their class at medical school? A doctor.

At some point the brain trust of doctors and nurses decided that maybe it wasn't colic, and my daughter was given IV fluids for dehydration. Naturally, they acted like they were doing her a huge favor. Yeah, a *favor*—which, after I received the bill, will always be referred to as "the favor that ate up my daughter's college tuition." A day later she was completely fine. I, however, needed a good six months to get my blood pressure down to normal. But what's worse, much worse than your run-of-the-mill sick baby is when your kid is sick and no one can figure out what's wrong.

A year later, when my daughter was two, I was gliding through life on just a whisper of Zoloft, registering for and dismissing preschools based on their smell and deciding whether or not dark red nail polish is too whorish for a mom (my official answer: It's not), when one day my toddler, of the insanely cute banter and boundless energy, woke up with a fever and wouldn't walk. Not wanting to be overprotective, I decided to wait a little while and see if she would pencil walking into her schedule after a teaspoon of Motrin. But by noon, she still wouldn't put any weight on her feet, so I called the pediatrician.

My husband and I brought her in "right away," as we were told to do by a receptionist with a worried voice. This is never a good sign. Receptionists can usually maintain a flat affect even when being told that their hair's on fire. After examining her, the on-call doctor made a preliminary diagnosis of toxic synovitis.

"Sounds much scarier than it is," she said with a smile. "It's really a complication of the common cold that a lot of young kids get. But by tomorrow she should be fine as wine."

We breathed a sigh of relief.

"But if not, bring her to urgent care, because she'll need to be evaluated further." She threw that last part in as we handed over our next car payment to their billing clerk.

The next day our daughter was not fine. In fact, her fever was high and she was still in no mood to be upright. I nervously paged my pediatrician to see what he thought. Unfortunately, my pediatrician was spending his weekend giving physicals to kids who were auditioning to be cast on a kids' reality show. Again, I live in L.A. But my pediatrician, whom you may have heard me shamelessly brag about before, is such a saint that he told me to bring her on down to the Doubletree Hotel, where right past the jazz atrium he'd pimped out a suite into a makeshift examination room. Oh yeah, there was a scale and everything.

On the downside, he couldn't figure out what was wrong and sent us to urgent care for more tests. On the upside, unlike our doctor's office, the Doubletree validated our parking.

After a ninety-minute wait surrounded by ill but walking children and healthy but angry parents, we finally got in to see the doctor at urgent care. Let me say this, I'm normally fairly laid-back when it comes to my child. I don't cut up her hot dogs into a gazillion pieces for fear of choking, nor do I chase her around the playground yelling, "Be careful . . . careful . . . CAREFUL," but this doctor took me from a four to a ten in the anxiety department in record time. He opened with, "This is very, very serious" and closed with, "could be childhood leukemia." In between were "septic hip," "bone infection," and a few others, but all my husband and I heard was blah, blah, blah, CHILDHOOD LEUKEMIA.

We were rushed to the hospital to be admitted overnight for tests. To say my daughter's a pussy when it comes to taking blood would be an understatement, but to say that I'm a pussy when it comes to my daughter experiencing an ounce of pain would be a *huge* understatement. My husband accompanied her into the treatment room for an IV and blood test. An hour and half later, she was sobbing uncontrollably, I was sobbing uncontrollably, and the male nurse was sweating so much he could've filled four Big Gulps. He couldn't get the blood no matter how much he tortured her—and he blamed her. Apparently she was too "anxious." Really? Experiencing anxiety while being held down in an impersonal room under attack from needles and fluorescent lights? That does seem strange! It was traumatizing and unsuccessful—much like bikini shopping is for me.

Seeing as our room was about the size of a department store changing room, my husband and I calmed ourselves with *National Enquirer* stories of Anna Nicole's untimely demise in the hallway while our daughter slept in the one bed. At seven a.m. the doctor arrived to inform us that they *still* needed blood. What were these people, vampires? I argued with the doctor that my daughter needed something to calm her down before being subjected to another round of needles. Perhaps to calm *me* down, they decided to give her a little dose of something called Versed. Unless you live in a country where alcohol is routinely served to the preschool set, this is the closest you will ever get to seeing your kid drunk. My daughter acted like a tipsy sorority chick on *Girls Gone Wild*, ripping off her T-shirt and practically begging the nurse to take her blood. I guess it's some good shit. If anyone knows where to locate it on the black market, I'm in.

A few hours later we were told that all her blood

work came back clean and it had just been toxic synovitis all along. And really, I think toxic synovitis is probably a medical term for "she just didn't feel like walking for a day or two." I would have been more pissed, but by then my peanut was not only walking but, clad only in a diaper, she was running into other kids' rooms, attempting to scale a blood pressure machine in the hallway, and touching all the painted pictures of crabs and seahorses on the wall. I think we were discharged moments before she would've contracted a mean staph infection.

For a long time I appreciated every second with my daughter even more than I had before, if that's even possible. Every time I looked at her, I thanked God that she was healthy, that I'd chosen to have a child in the first place. That is, until four days later when, now full of energy, she used a Scripto Ultima black ink pen to draw pictures all over the beige bathroom wall.

I can't argue that there's nothing worse than your child getting sick, but the fact is, they do get sick—a lot. I don't care if you wash your hands more than Monk, never go more than five minutes without wiping something down with an antibacterial cloth, or even keep your kid in a plastic bubble. If there's a germ, they'll find it. The best we can do is to try to stay calm and not jump to the conclusion that they are dying of a rare disease every time they have a slight cough. I know; easier said than done. Children should come with a warning label and a prescription for Versed. Just my opinion.

Movin' On Up
to the Big Bed

When my daughter was about two years old and change, it dawned on me that having conversations with someone who spoke in complete sentences through the bars of a crib was getting a little ridiculous—she was three feet tall and could *almost* tell a knock-knock joke. Could it be time for a real bed? But moving to a grown-up bed seemed so drastic. What would stop her from just getting up anytime she didn't feel like taking a nap, which was every day? It seemed way too early for her to have that kind of freedom. On the other hand, it would be nice not to have to go get her if she was thirsty or had a bad dream. It would save me a whole three steps across the hall. Why exercise if you don't have to?

I'll be honest, for all my decision-making bravado, I'm not above asking a more seasoned mom for guidance on these topics. The problem is, most answers you get when you solicit advice are all over the place. At a group playdate I put the "when to move to a big bed" question out to the other mothers, sat back, and waited for enlightenment.

One mom told me with great authority that unless my child was climbing out of her crib and endangering herself, I should go ahead and keep her in there as long as possible. *What does that mean?* I wondered. "As long as possible" seemed a bit vague. *Until she enters grade school? Gets her learner's permit? Hires an attorney to sue me for false imprisonment?* Another mom had this bit of brilliance: "Go ahead and get her a bed, but put a baby gate on her door so she can't leave." Oh good, so now her crib is the size of her bedroom, and if she cries at night I still have to go free her from her pen. A third mom just glared at me like I was asking when my daughter would be old enough to pose for child pornography. "Her own bed? I'm sorry, but I'm the wrong person to ask. Sydney Rose has shared a bed with Mommy and Daddy since she was born and she's fourteen. I see absolutely no reason to make a child sleep all by themselves. It's mean!" Oh God, I should've known—there's a die-hard family-bedder in every bunch. At that point I decided to shelve the whole project and wait for divine intervention.

A few months later, after a few friends of mine had purchased their first toddler beds, my husband and I brought up the notion of a big-girl bed to our daughter. She got so excited you'd have thought Dora just popped by for brunch. We had an inkling that the time had come. The next week we headed to Ikea, test-drove a few adorable convertibles (they expand from toddler size to twin), took one home, and my husband attempted to set that sucker up. Two hours, fifty "fuck this's," and one possibly sprained toe later, our daughter crawled into a white wrought-iron big-girl bed, snuggled with her purple blanket, and claimed it as her own—promptly moving me to tears and my husband to an allergy attack, which sure seemed a lot like tears, but he assured me it was *just allergies*.

Knowing that some kids need to revisit the crib—sort of like an inmate who, after serving a thirty-spot behind bars in Cook County, suddenly gets paroled and finds he can't adapt to life on the outside (I really need to stop watching *Shawshank Redemption* every time it's shown on cable)—we decided to strip the crib but leave it inside her room for a while. Turns out it was completely unnecessary, because after a few nights of being a grown-up, she pronounced that cribs are for babies and banished it from her bedroom forever.

So was I right to be concerned that my daughter would be tempted to borrow the car keys and head out for a nightcap the second she realized she was free to do so? Yes and no. It wasn't quite as bad as I feared, yet not as perfect a transition as I'd hoped. At first I don't think she realized that there was nothing keeping her from getting up. My husband and I would peek in on her at night before she fell asleep and watch her suspiciously eyeing the perimeter of the bed, like a dog surrounded by an electronic fence. We stood in the hallway and gloated—albeit quietly, so as not to disturb her. Our gloating turned out to be a bit hasty.

It took a week or so, but she eventually figured out that there were no longer wooden bars keeping her from her books, her toys, and most importantly, her mom and dad's bed. The first night I opened my eyes at four a.m. just as her head popped fuzzily into view, it scared the crap out of me. I had made the fatal error of removing my contacts before bed, and through my compromised vision, my daughter, in her bright pink Elmo nightie and slept-on curly hair, looked more like a midget in a clown suit. For a second I was worried I was trapped in a Stephen King novella.

"Mama, I want some milk" (fine, juice if you must know). I got up like a zombie, fetched her a cup of milk, and led her sleepily back to her bed, but the requests kept coming: "I wanna sleep in your bed. Can I have one more story? I need a corn dog." The kid has a corn dog obsession that apparently doesn't even let up when she sleeps. After a few consecutive nights of nocturnal visits and requests, I realized that if I kept giving in, no one would be sleeping until she and her corn dog obsession careened out of control and left to travel the state fair circuit, so I limited her to a cup of water and a kiss. Eventually, after a few nights of crying, we all started sleeping through the night again, and my husband and I resumed gloating in earnest. Seriously, what's it going to take for us to learn?

Sure enough, after a few weeks of relative calm, we started getting more four a.m. visits, but this time she would just climb into our bed and promptly fall back asleep. We were so surprised the first few times, we just let her stay. Unfortunately, I found that although she continued to snooze soundly, I, the recipient of numerous kicks to the face, found it challenging to sleep and maintain a zone defense simultaneously. We came upon a compromise: She had to stay in bed until it was light out, and then she could sleep with us the last hour or two. And that's worked out well—except for maybe the unaccounted-for end of daylight saving time. But luckily, we didn't gloat this time.

I realize that some parents find their toddler's transition to the big bed tougher than Macaulay Culkin's transition to puberty. My good friend Irene made the fatal error of moving her two-year-old daughter to a big bed very early because she could hurl herself out of her crib at ten months. Ever since she could walk, she's gotten up nightly to wander the house for hours once her poor parents are asleep. She's been known to empty drawers of clothes, hide CDs in every corner of the house, and polish off all the Mint Milanos, but on the bright side, sometimes she rearranges the furniture quite tastefully. I guess in some cases baby gates aren't quite the psycho suggestion I made them out to be. My bad.

Another mom found the switch to the big bed to be so unnerving to her high-strung toddler, who was never a great sleeper to begin with, that she ended up having to return to the bad old days of driving her little boy around town all night like an infant just to get him to doze off. I don't know how it all turned out, because she's currently in rehab battling a horrible NoDoz addiction.

Thank God, most of us get through the transition to grown-up bed without permanent scars, and really, what else are you gonna do? You can't stand in the way of progress. I have to tell you, there's nothing like watching my daughter lying in her big-girl bed—little head on little Swedish Ikea pillow like a real live adult—to remind me how fast they grow up. It seems like one minute they're lying in their cribs helpless as a hammered Nick Nolte, watching their mobile spin round and round, and the next minute they're clutching an FAO Schwarz stuffed English Bulldog and demanding bedding with higher thread count! That's when it really hits you that having children is a costly endeavor.

Food: It's Not What's for Dinner

When I was a kid, I hated onions with a passion normally reserved for terrorists and tobacco companies. I also despised Brussels sprouts, broccoli, spinach (fine, all green vegetables, yes, I'm talking to you, kale!), mushrooms, quiche, lasagna (because you never knew if onions could be lurking in that mess), tomatoes, olives, Swiss cheese, liver (duh), blueberries, pickles, sweet potatoes, and chicken (except the skin). I hated entire food groups! I guess I was what you'd call a picky eater. What *did* I eat, you ask? The usual toddler staples: fish sticks, grilled cheese, pasta with *plain* tomato sauce (read ketchup), all snack cakes by Hostess, and frog's legs (my Sunday dad took me to expensive French restaurants after my parents' divorce).

So did I turn out to be a vegetable-hating, frog-leg-nibbling adult? Of course not. Well, truth be told, I still won't go near pâté, no matter how clever the presentation, and I hate onions with nearly the same intensity, but I no longer let my negative feelings stand in the way of enjoying an otherwise perfectly tasty lasagna. The way I see it, my eating habits as a child weren't that different from most, and yet I turned out to be quite a healthy adult. But loads of parents are obsessed with their toddler's picky eating habits.

Some kids will eat just about anything when they're babies. And the mothers of those babies love to tell you about it as if it somehow is a reflection of their superior parenting skills. One particularly irksome new mom friend would actually call to update me on all the unusual foods her daughter was enjoying, patting herself on the back for her daughter's sophisticated palate as if it was genetic.

One evening I answered the phone to this: "You won't believe what Little Miss International is eating right now: a crispy baguette topped with red pepper hummus. Hummus is her very favorite food! Isn't it amazing?" she crowed. I didn't find it so amazing. What I did find amazing was that I still took this bizzotch's calls. You'll feel better knowing that now that her daughter's a toddler, the halcyon days of hummus are behind her. She's lucky if she can convince Little Miss International to eat a piece of American cheese.

It's typical of toddlers to become insanely selective in their likes and dislikes once they realize they have free will. The power to decide what goes into their mouths is heady stuff indeed for a child who's still outweighed four to one by their parents, and they will take full advantage of their newfound authority. It's normal for a kid to eschew entire food groups; it's normal for them to eat the same food over and over for a month—hey, it worked for Elvis—and it's normal for them to go an entire day eating nothing but a peanut M&M they found on the floor of the car. What I don't think is normal or healthy is the insane power struggles that erupt over a kid who won't eat his veggies. As much as you'd like to, you can't control it. The only thing you can control is your reaction.

In a misguided attempt to get their kids to eat a meal, some parents turn their child's fairly normal behavior into a full-blown power struggle, refusing to prepare a tasty alternative when three-year-old Emma doesn't want to taste the Sweet Ragout of Quince and Lamb her mama so lovingly prepared for the whole family.

"I made Sweet Ragout of Quince and Lamb and that is exactly what you'll be eating," she declares when little Emma refuses and asks for peanut butter and jelly. "If you don't want the Sweet Ragout of Quince and Lamb, then fine, but I will not make you a separate meal! You can just wait until tomorrow."

That plan of attack probably won't get Emma to eat her dinner, but if her mom keeps it up, it may help Emma fit back into her twelve-month-old clothes pretty quick. Great job! Stick with it and eventually Emma may get into a preemie onesie! Go for the gold.

I'm not saying the other extreme is any better. Nothing makes a child want to taste something less than a parent chasing them around with a forkful of pasta say-ing, "Come on, taste this. Just give it a try. Come on, one little bite. Please, please, *please?* Do it for Daddy!" Collapsing in a pool of tears when your toddler isn't in the mood for a snack will only cause everyone involved unnecessary anxiety.

There's something to be said for not turning your kitchen into a diner and preparing fourteen different plates, like you're auditioning for an episode of *Top Chef,* based on your child's mercurial appetite. If you've offered something they like and they still refuse to eat, it cer-tainly won't kill them to miss a meal. Come to think of it, the same goes for most adults—especially me.

If you're really dead set on getting your kids to eat some vegetables, I won't try to talk you out of it. There are women who've been known to go to incredible lengths just to get a single stalk of broccoli introduced into their child's system. If you want to blend some greenery into a thin puree then add it to pancake batter and see if it will pass for edible after you've smothered it with maple syrup and butter, then by all means, make a morning of it. I'd prefer to watch the *Today Show.* I just have to won-der how much satisfaction you'll feel when your fussy eater takes one bite of their grayish pancake imposter and flings the rest of it against the wall.

While some parents worry about whether their toddlers are eating enough, other parents waste valuable time obsessing on whether they're eating too much. Most kids, when being offered a variety of reasonably healthy foods (and reasonably healthy does not include a steady stream of Doritos and Dr Pepper) will eat as much as they need. Unless your pediatrician seems concerned or your eighteen-month-old gets recruited for one of Maury Povich's "Big Baby" shows, you probably don't need to be so overly focused on their weight. In fact, if your two-year-old is actually interested enough in eating their mashed potatoes to ask for seconds, and your technique is to say, "Don't be piggy, I think you've had enough," just know that I think you're ridiculous and you have just ensured that your child will go on to weigh three hundred pounds. Kudos.

Along with trying to control portion size, some militant mamas eliminate sweets altogether. I call them the Sugar Objectors—you know, those moms who try to pass off raisins as "nature's candy" and never allow processed sugar into the house? This will always backfire. We've all known fat adults who grew up in a house exactly like this. It works like a charm until the kid gets an allowance and quickly becomes best friends with the ice-cream man. Great. Now you've created a sugar-deprived monster whose constant companion is a possible child molester who drives around in a creepy van all day. And really, didn't we all love candy so much as kids that we were 100 percent sure we'd own a candy store when we grew up? And how many of us actually own that candy store now? I loved McDonald's, too—but I don't own a McDonald's franchise, nor did I attend McDonald's Hamburger University, which I swore I would. Although that should be blamed less on my lack of love for McDonald's and more on my lack of follow-through and the fact that I don't do well on tests.

Don't get sucked into comparing yourself with other mothers about what their tykes may or may not be eating. Some women act like the food struggle is a competitive sport. We've all been confronted with Food Fakers at the park or on playdates, who seem to have no trouble getting their little ones to not only eat but suck down healthy snacks—*seem* being the operative word. Food Fakers whip out their Tupperware containers filled with steamed vegetables, melba toast, and multivitamins with so much fanfare you'd think they were putting on a Broadway show. Want to feel better? Next time, instead of turning back to your Goldfish pretzels in shame, keep watching. I, for one, have never actually seen a kid eating any of the delicacies the Food Fakers have so meticulously prepared. But I have seen quite a few organic asparagus stalks buried in the sand.

So what's a parent who's worried about their toddler's eating habits to do? The only advice I've heard that makes sense is to offer semihealthy fare one food at a time without being overly invested in it. You don't want your child to miss out on something they might actually enjoy due to lack of opportunity. Think back to things you once liked. On a hunch, I served my roughage-challenged daughter raw cauliflower and Green Goddess salad dressing, and shockingly, she devoured it. I was so excited I almost spilled the chocolate milkshake I was using to bribe her. I'm kidding—the milkshake was all mine. Of course, the next time I offered up cauliflower she had a good long laugh at my foolhardiness and went back to her Pirate's Booty, shaking her head as if to say, "I'm just going to pretend that never happened."

Keep in mind that picky eating is a phase that all kids go through—a long phase that may last several decades, but a phase nonetheless. The fickle quality of a toddler's taste buds never ceases to amaze me. My daughter went from loving Kraft Macaroni & Cheese so much she would've happily eaten it for breakfast, lunch, and dinner every day to acting like the good people of Kraft murdered Elmo. I was buying it so often I figured I'd rent a pickup truck and get a gross of it at Costco. Naturally, that was the exact same day mac & cheese became public enemy number one. So now I'm the proud owner of a year's supply of mac & cheese and we can no longer fit both of our cars in the garage.

All you can do is ride out the next few years, set a good example, and celebrate the little food victories here and there. So before you spend a boatload of money on pricey books telling you what to do about your fussy eater or even offering recipes, know that your toddler will eventually expand their culinary horizons on their own schedule—they all do—and before long you'll have something brand-new to openly panic about.

One last warning: Don't finish your child's meals for them. Pizza, pasta, and grilled cheese are, let's just say, not staples of any calorie reduction plan. I learned this the hard way. After a few months of "assisting" my daughter to see how delicious mac & cheese is if you just give it another chance, I managed to pack on about fifteen pounds. My daughter never did start eating it again, but I ended up getting a little more use out of my maternity clothes. Looks like the person whose food consumption I should have been most concerned about was my own.

What's On Your Toddler's PalmPilot?

The other day I caught sight of a truly terrifying sight: A mother of a little girl in my daughter's preschool class opened her day planner, and I realized it was her three-year-old's schedule of after-nursery-school enrichment courses. What the hell? How many activities was her toddler doing in one day that would take up her own page in a daily day planner? *Why not just go ahead and get Little Miss Overachiever her own PalmPilot?* I didn't say this out loud because I didn't want to give the mom any Christmas present ideas.

For approximately two seconds I felt completely inadequate. I was under the impression that after a few hours of gluing macaroni on construction paper, spray painting it gold, and then tracing her hand a few dozen times, the only thing on my kid's agenda should be a nap. If I go to bed early enough to knock the latest episode of *The Biggest Loser* off my TiVo queue, I feel like I've accomplished something—and hell, if I manage to throw in the last of my *Access Hollywood*s I feel downright smug! So maybe

I'm not the picture of ambition. But then I snapped back to irritation—these are toddlers we're talking about! Isn't downtime their God-given right?

It's no secret that the pubescent kids of our generation have a lot more on their plate than a few zits and an unrequited crush on a sexy teacher's assistant. Today's tweens are living in a more overscheduled and pressurized environment than your typical Wall Streeter. Between hours of homework and all the extracurricular activities to look good for prospective colleges (junior varsity basketball, golf, soccer, painting scenery for *Macbeth*, Spirit Squad, jazz band, running for class treasurer, and then donating every extra minute to Habitat for Humanity to show they are "involved in their community"), it's no wonder kids are pilfering their parent's pot and engaging in heavy petting on school buses. Although, unlike when I was young, most of these kids don't even have chores ("Hey, Harvard ain't looking at how well you vacuum, son.").

It's bad enough that our tweens are this stressed, but do we now have to throw our little toddlers into the rat race? I'm not saying that our little ones should never take any classes. I understand that the brain drain of raising a toddler can inspire you to throw your kid into a few harmless activities to alleviate boredom in both of you and give you the opportunity to interact with a few adults. There's no shame in admitting that listening to most long toddler conversations is slightly less scintillating than watching professional bowling. Actually, it's more like watching QVC, since little kids always sound like they're trying to sell you stuff: *You wanna go to the toy store, Mama? Would that be fun? Huh? Let's go there, Mama! You like purple? I love purple. Izzat your favorite color, Mama? Is purple your favorite color? Purple is your favorite color, Mama! I need for purple to be your favorite color!* A few hours of this and you'll be taking your prescription cough medicine way past the point of being symptomatic. I get it.

Sure, you can sit on the floor stringing beads, coloring, re-enacting entire *Batman* episodes, making banana bread together, and reading *The Chronicles of Narnia* for a few hours . . . or until you realize that those few hours were in actuality only five minutes. So trying to keep busy is understandable, but be sure you're doing it for the right reasons. Yes, a baby basketball class or some Tiny Tot T-ball action can be a nice break in the monotony. But if you've signed your two-year-old up for daily T-ball practice in a competitive league, ask yourself: Is it really for fun or am I overinvested in my little tiger getting a chubby leg up in the world? Is he blowing off some steam or "building his portfolio" for college?

Some of these classes don't even make sense. If your one-year-old is enrolled in Italian for Pre-Walkers, you'd better either be fluent in the language or planning to move to Florence. Barring that, you'll have to send him off to some kind of toddler exchange program so he can practice with a native family while you entertain little Giuseppe, who zips around your living room on his moped and speed-dials Papa John's delivery. Otherwise your kid will lose everything he's learned quicker than you can say *ciao*.

Swimming's another one that seems a little ridiculous. According to the American Academy of Pediatrics, children aren't physically capable of truly learning to swim until age four, but that doesn't stop hordes of parents from signing their two-year-old up for intensive lessons. In L.A., you're nobody until you've hired the biker swim coach. Legend has it that trendy L.A. parents hire this hardcore dude to zoom up on a Harley and implement the "scared straight" method of teaching kids to swim: If they're crying, he unceremoniously dunks their little heads under the water. For, like, five hundred bucks he guarantees they'll be able to swim in five days. And I can pretty much guarantee you'll end up spending a hundred times that for intensive therapy. What's the rush? The Summer Olympics are still a few years off.

I must admit, I do bring my daughter to the cutest ballet/tap class once a week—or more accurately, once every three weeks, when I catch sight of her adorable pink tights in her drawer and remember we haven't gone in a while. She gets such a kick out of sashaying across the room in her tutu with a pair of kitty ears on her head and pompoms in each hand while loosely learning first position. And it's no use fronting here, I spent twenty-seven dollars on a pair of black patent-leather tap shoes for her—even though I can't think of a single cool person who tap dances, except possibly Savion Glover—and really, isn't he more cool-adjacent?

My friend who runs the dance studio tells me that parents these days aren't satisfied with their two- and three-year-olds just taking the class—no, they have to perform! Jazz hands! They will not sign up for a class unless it culminates in a recital. It doesn't matter to some of these overcaffeinated crazies that their kids are too young to master *Swan Lake*. This is not about the kids; it's about the moms, who stand behind their kids pantomiming pointe work like some kind of pudgy Anna Pavlova wannabe. Listen, ladies, if you want to take ballet, then *you* do it, but don't make your toddlers live your dreams. They have dreams of their own. They long to look at a picture of a butterfly for a half hour or jump up and down to a Laurie Berkner song. Listen, I took gymnastics in grade school, and yes, in my mind I'm pretty sure with just a little more training and a little less drinking I could be back handspringing circles around Nadia Comaneci in no time, but I'm not going to do it! My time is done. And so is yours.

Studies say that too much activity can be damaging to a young child anyway. Overscheduling not only hampers a toddler's creativity and ability to entertain himself, but it can also overstimulate him. What ever happened to letting kids use their imagination? Instead of forcing classes on them, try to think back to your own toddlerhood. Remember when riding your tricycle around the block looking for rocks was cool? Followed by taking a break to pop some buttered Wonder Bread in the toaster oven, taking it out with a fork, and then going back outside to find a rock? Now some parents aren't happy unless their kid is out rappelling off rocks.

Kids don't need a da Vinci art class, kiddie calculus, or tuba lessons. And if you can brag that your three-year-old is a black belt in karate, you don't deserve to be congratulated, you deserve to be taken in for questioning.

So you have your four-year-old in what you feel is a reasonable number of activities, you're letting them have some downtime, and they *seem* happy to you, but you're still wondering if they're doing too much. How do you know? Well, for one thing you can always check their MySpace page. And then if they have a MySpace page, it means *they're doing too much!* So let's all agree right now to save the BlackBerries, PalmPilots, and other PDAs until at least their fifth birthday. It'll save us all money, and it'll give them something to look forward to. As for my daughter, I'm trying to steer away from the insanity and toward my brand of lofty goal making. I think it's working. Last night before bed she told me, "Mama, I rode my bike and I ate four cookies today!"

"I'm so proud of you, baby," I said, squeezing her up. "You did *a lot* for one day."

Signs Your Child May Be Suffering from Toddler Burnout

She still seems stressed *after* Kindergarten Kundalini
   Yoga

She starts yelling *"adios"* repeatedly to her Spanish
   teacher only two hours into her lesson.

He doesn't even seem the least bit excited about finding
   a rare Cymatium pyrum seashell at the beach.

She passive-aggressively makes you late to take her to
   her third soccer game of the day.

He claims to have "misplaced" the piano right when it's
   time to practice.

He seems almost disappointed that he got into honors
   preschool math.

She tells *you* it's time for her nap.

The Potty: Revisited

Closing the deal on potty training was one of the more Byzantine processes on the parenting agenda. We'd been straddling the fence for a while, my kid and I. She knew how to use her little potty, the one we'd ceremoniously bought together and covered with princess stickers—and which now sat decoratively in our bathroom—but mostly she found diapers just as capable of doing the job and a lot more convenient. And let's be honest, I found diapers to be pretty damn convenient too.

My pediatrician told me that eighteen months was the right age to potty train, and I had bought the damn thing, right? I just didn't see the wisdom in pushing the issue. One day she'd pee in her potty, and then for three days I'd forget about even asking her until the next time I had to shell out another forty dollars for diapers. Eventually I decided that something should be done to at least get us moving in the right direction, so I purchased Pull-Ups potty-training pants.

Pull-Ups are training diapers that boast "feel and learn" technology. According to the box with the picture of a happy toddler, arms raised in victory as he has apparently pulled that diaper down around his ankles and taken the party train to potty town, they are the quickest road to leading a diaper-free existence. Not for us; if my daughter remained naked from at least the waist down, she held it in. But if a pair of Pull-Ups was on, she found it to be quite absorbent enough for her needs, thank you very much, and like a drunk frat guy at an outdoor keg party, she'd pee pretty much anywhere. Unfortunately, remaining naked from the waist down wasn't a workable option for either of us, at least out in public (most especially frowned on at the public library, it turns out), and short of moving to a nudist resort I was out of ideas, so our potty-training mission stalled out a bit. I figured it would happen in its own time when she was ready.

We cruised along like that for a while: peeing in the potty at home and using diapers when we went out. I made a couple of halfhearted attempts to get her to use a public bathroom, but she was scared of the cavernous echo of a department store ladies' room, afraid to sit on a grown-up-size seat, and somehow worried about being accidentally flushed away. Gosh, I have no idea where she would get a crazy fear like that. Oh wait, yes I do—thanks, DreamWorks. We probably would have happily continued on our slow, merry, diaper-wearing way if preschool hadn't started breathing down our necks with their draconian potty-training rules that flew in the face of my decidedly lazier parenting style.

We weren't the only ones in this predicament. Most of my mom friends were facing this at the same time and having the same amount of trouble taking potty training from half-assed to full-on. With preschool only about six weeks off, I was suddenly feeling a bit desperate.

That's when I decided to make my move and pull out the big guns: underpants. What could be more persuasive than a pair of adorable new cotton panties? This was actually a win-win, because it combined potty training *and* shopping. I let her pick them out herself, and she smartly went with a *Curious George, Happy Feet,* and *Little Mermaid* assortment—which (note to the manufacturer) should come with a complimentary hankie, because nothing brings on the tears like the first time you witness a toddler butt in a pair of Ariel undies. When it comes to pivotal moments in motherhood, this one is *way* up there. Ironically, it's one of the *least* appropriate moments to capture on video and immediately post on YouTube.

Once in her "big girl underpants," I felt my daughter was ready to take the potty-training world by storm— just not too far from home.

And then I ran into my friend Julie in the produce section of Ralph's, where we were both shopping with our toddler daughters. While we stopped to catch up, her daughter suddenly let loose a stream of urine on the floor. I was shocked—not that her daughter peed on the floor, but that my friend was daring enough to take her out with no diaper on. I'd seen this friend only a couple of weeks earlier and knew that her kid was nowhere near potty trained. So while the Ralph's employee took care of "cleanup, aisle one," I begged her for the full scoop.

"Oh yeah, we threw the diapers out last week for good. Just went for it," she told me.

"Cold turkey?" This woman deserved some kind of medal of bravery.

"Had to—those training diapers weren't doing the trick, and you know, we started preschool, so . . . we sort of had to."

"And it's working?" I started taking mental notes more seriously than a court stenographer.

"At first there were a lot of accidents. But it's getting better every day." We both averted our eyes from the freshly mopped spot on the floor.

"Yeah, yeah, but what about public bathrooms?" There had to be a catch, right? I wasn't going to let my daughter go down in the potty-training competition that easily.

"Well, right now I have to bring a little travel potty seat with me everywhere we go, but it fits in my purse, and since I bought it she will go in just about any bathroom." Jesus, my friend had covered all the angles.

And that's when I had an epiphany: The only one holding up my daughter's potty-training process was me. Perhaps due to the books and Internet advice I'd subjected myself to, I had thought that it was all about her readiness—thus the *Elmo Goes Potty* video we snuck into her vast regular Elmo collection and the *Once Upon a Potty* book she found amusing—once. But it turns out she *was* ready; I was the one who hadn't been ready. If I wanted us to move forward, *I* needed to get committed. So that very day (more realistically, sometime later the next week) I bought the purse-size potty seat, which isn't quite as discreet as my friend made it out to be—nothing says "mom" quite like carrying a toilet seat around with you, sort of like having a minivan hanging off your shoulder. But we did manage to stop wearing diapers during the day; thus began the actual hard work of potty training.

Not everyone is up to the task; I have it on very good authority that some people actually go so far as to hire a potty-training expert specifically to come in and toilet train their kid in a week or two. Yes, they actually farm out this unpleasant but integral part of parenting. Can you believe people do that? It's so insane! And so out of my price range!

For those of you who opt to go the do-it-yourself route, I can't say it was pretty. It's tougher than you'd think to constantly ask, "Do you need to go potty? What about now? What about now? How about now? Uh-oh . . . too late." You must always carry an extra change of clothes for your child (and you, and any random passerby), be ready to brave a Chevron station bathroom that should require a hazmat suit to enter, and above all, remain patient and consistent.

Of course, as with any major life change, we had setbacks, and you will experience them too: a sudden onslaught of accidents, a short stint back in diapers, or a new problem with constipation.

Even though my daughter was doing pretty well, there were certain times she insisted she that she needed to wear a diaper, and because she looked a little sad about it and I didn't know how to react, I would just pretend it was a fabulous idea! "A diaper? What, are you kidding me? But of course! Underpants are so five-minutes-ago. Pampers are de rigueur! Why would a fashion-forward toddler such as yourself want to be caught dead in Hello Kitty undies?" Okay, I may have overdone it a little, but I didn't want to point out that diapers were a negative thing any more than I'd want my husband pointing out that the giant baked potato I was eating probably wasn't part of my Atkins plan. So she needed the security of a diaper once in a while—so what? Was I inwardly freaking out? Just a bit. But as with so many other aspects of toddlers, I knew that her behavior was normal and that the best course of action was to just roll with it.

But just because *you* know that a little regression is normal, it may not prevent you from feeling defensive when other moms, mother-in-laws, or know-it-all neighbors attempt to put a little shame in your game. It's bound to happen; somewhere along the line your previously potty-trained toddler will get a few raised eyebrows for even the briefest return to diapers. But screw it, would they rather the alternative? Nothing puts other people more on edge than an *almost* potty-trained kid having a seat on their new couch or, God forbid, splashing around nude in their swimming pool. Just know that you're not alone. All kids go through this—if you don't trust me, ask any preschool teacher, expert, or honest other mom.

Bottom line: Wearing a diaper once in a while is not a reason to get professional help; unless, of course, you're a forty-three-year-old astronaut traveling at the speed of light to kill your ex-lover's new girlfriend. Then I'm afraid all bets are off.

Shear Madness

My daughter's first day of preschool was just two weeks away. We did a major trip to Target for a Hello Kitty backpack—all cool and black with pink straps and a subtle sparkly finish, definitely ensuring her membership with the preschool glitterati set. She also got a colored pencil set and a Snow White lunch box with matching dwarves thermos (which she'd been sleeping with in her bed every night since she'd made its acquaintance), plus we'd hit the Carter's outlet for a few new outfits, and potty training was sort of in the home stretch. Yup, my daughter was poised to become a preschool prodigy. There was just one thing missing: a haircut.

Personally, I'd always dreaded this event because my mother, who believed hair cutting was just a natural extension of her so-called sewing abilities, thought it was perfectly fine and a great money-saver to pull out the old Singer sewing scissors and chop away. The woman wasn't satisfied until I had a straight wall of bangs well above my eyebrows. It wasn't until I was in the sixth grade, after years of begging and pleading, that my mother finally agreed to get me a professional cut. Only it wasn't at a salon per se, it was a friend's mom who cut hair out of her house on the cheap while enjoying a few gin and grapefruit juices—But hey, I thought, at least it wasn't my mom. That cut left me with a version of the much-sought-after Dorothy Hamill that was dangerously closer to a Mark Hamill.

Given my past trauma, I would've just let my kid's hair go long, but even though she has the cutest naturally curly hair you've ever seen, its growth wasn't following any plan approved by nature and was quickly becoming a 'fro.

Hoping to spare my daughter the Singer sewing scissors routine that had plagued my youth, I figured the least I could do for my daughter's future self-esteem would be to let only someone with actual scissor know-how anywhere near her hair.

It turns out that kiddie hair salons are a growing trend, and you can find a place that specializes in lopping off children's locks almost anywhere. I was excited because I'd heard that these hair salons for children typically offer movies, toys, and the promise of a balloon to keep kids busy and prevent unnecessary meltdowns. I thought this was genius! And why stop there? Why not do that in adult salons? I know that during my last hair appointment, watching *The Devil Wears Prada*, snacking on a chocolate croissant, and sipping a glass of bourbon would've gone a long way to take my mind off the fact that I walked out of there looking like the newest member of the Bay City Rollers.

So I set out to find a cute kids' chop shop near me for my daughter's inaugural cut, but I wasn't prepared for the wave of nausea that overtook me when my Google search for kids' salons also turned up a slew of kid spas that cater to toddlers, tweens, and teens, offering manicures, pedicures, massage, formal hairdos, Mystic tan, and a host of other amenities. Hold the phone. Toddlers? Does a three-year-old really need an exfoliating seaweed wrap? Isn't their skin new enough as it is? And what exactly is so stressful about a kindergartner's lifestyle that they could possibly need a ninety-minute, 180-dollar relaxation massage? And call me prickly, but I don't ever want to hear a precocious seven-year-old compare the merits of acrylic nails versus artificial gels. Is it me? Am I the asshole?

Feeling decidedly less giddy, I chose a kid-friendly hair-cutting place in my neighborhood that featured all the bells and whistles, plus the cost-efficient price of twenty bucks, and hoped for the best.

From the minute we sat down in the waiting area, I knew I'd made a mistake—no matter where you looked, there were endless stuffed animal, colorful barrette, and flavored lip gloss buying opportunities, which I guess was supposed to make up for the lack of current gossip rags for me. After thirty minutes of staring into space listening to my daughter whine, "I want a toy, I want a toy," I would've been ecstatic to see a back issue of *Golf Digest*.

I was dangerously close to purchasing the little lady some apple-scented detangler and a floral Afro pick and calling it a day when our names were called. Too bad the wait ended up being the best part of the whole unmitigated disaster. The hairdresser, a guy mysteriously costumed as Edward Scissorhands, greeted us and reached out a plastic-scissored hand to my kid to lead her to his station. My daughter, not getting the early nineties reference, started crying, and she continued bawling sporadically for the rest of the appointment.

Minutes later my wet-cheeked daughter was seated in an adjustable-height mini yellow racecar chair, where she gripped the steering wheel for dear life as Eddie draped a plastic zebra wrap around her neck, pulled out a spray bottle of water, and started squirting down her hair. Watching my baby's worried little face almost made me nostalgic for the sewing scissors. *Almost.* But I kept my eyes on the prize—a daughter who would have stylish, non-laughed-at hair. Little did I know that the one I really should have been worried about was me.

"So what are we looking to do here today?" Scissorhands asked me while my daughter sat teary-eyed staring at *Shrek the Third* being projected on a big-screen TV.

"I guess just a trim. She's never had her hair cut before, and it's getting a bit unmanageable." Scissorhands held up a sixteenth of an inch of her hair through two fingers.

"About this much?"

"Um, you could probably go shorter than that." *For twenty bucks I'd like to actually be able to tell it's been cut.* He moved his fingers down an indiscernible amount.

"That's fine, I guess." But this didn't satisfy him. He needed to know if she wore her hair parted, to which side, and did she plan to style it with mousse. I felt like saying, "Jesus. She's three! Just cut it already!"

When Eddie *finally* got my daughter's cut underway, he turned his attention to me. "Honey, I can see a little gray in your hair. Do you dye it?"

"No." And come on! When you cut toddlers' hair, everyone over four is gonna look old. Of course, now I was starting to worry. *Shit, last I checked I had maybe two strands of gray, which I meticulously plucked out.*

Without looking away from me, he repositioned my daughter's face to the TV screen and told her to hold still. "You should really let me color that, or at least get a nice herbal rinse to get rid of that ugly gray. Have you considered highlights? At your age, you could definitely use a little light around your face to lift it up."

I was too stunned to say, "Listen, I'm only forty, and for your information a lot of people tell me I could easily pass for very late thirties—and furthermore, I don't need style advice from a guy who dresses up as an early nineties Johnny Depp character and cuts hair for kids who are still in diapers for a living." But it didn't matter because although it had barely been five minutes, he was done with my daughter's hair, which pretty much looked the same, only wetter.

"Are you ready for a blow-dry?" he asked, whipping the blow-dryer off its hook. My daughter looked at me and I looked at him like he'd just pulled out a .45 . Blow-dry? Had this freak ever met a toddler before? The sound of a blow-dryer scares the hell out of most of them, and the extra cost definitely scared the hell out of me!

"No, thanks. I think we're all good here."

"Are you sure? It's included in the thirty-five-dollar price."

"I thought a kid's haircut was twenty?"

"Oh that price list is six months old." Gee, thanks for the heads-up.

"Hey, I have an idea: How about you put up the correct price list and then I'll give you the corresponding amount of money? Sorry, but I'm a little anal, and the money that leaves my purse has to match the sign." After my little outburst, he quietly put the blow-dryer away and handed my daughter an old, pink, hair-covered balloon that had been sitting on the floor near her chair gathering dust and static electricity, and we finally headed for the exit, passing a little Down syndrome boy in a Batmobile chair screaming his head off. *I'm so with you, little man*, I thought. I felt a little bit like crying myself. I tried to catch the kid's eye to show him that he and I were truly simpatico on this place, but his mother gave me a stern look like she'd caught me staring inappropriately, so I quickly turned away. There was nothing left to do but whip out my credit card.

To add insult to injury, after the haircut fiasco, we ended up having to go to Baskin-Robbins for a couple of ice-cream sundaes just to get over our mutual trauma. The final tally for the ten-minute haircut: sixty-five dollars. It broke down like this:

> Buying toys and barrettes so kid won't cry . . . as much: $20
> Haircut (including unused blow-dry): $35
> Soothing after-cut treats: $10
> Getting out of there without committing homicide: *Priceless*.

I have a sneaking suspicion that there is a shiny pair of Singer sewing scissors in my daughter's future. Let's just hope the Dorothy Hamill comes back in style soon.

Preschool Psychosis

I went to preschool a long, long time ago, you know, like fifteen or sixteen years ago, so I may not be remembering this right, but I could swear that learning how to fold a newspaper into a pointy hat, molding a little Play-Doh, bouncing around on a Hoppity Hop for a spell, and then breaking for Saltines and lemon-lime Kool-Aid seemed to be the order of the day. True, I didn't turn out to be a Rhodes scholar, but I can make my own party hats out of the *LA Weekly*—so there's that. But after I had a baby of my own, I found out that times had changed drastically.

The politics of preschool has gotten way out of control. Parents these days could easily spend the better part of every day discussing the ins and outs of different school curriculums: public vs. private, progressive, Ivy League track, Wiccan vs. Coven. People, please! It's freaking preschool, not premed. Your child's whole future is not riding on whether or not you go with the Reggio Emilia method versus Montessori. I'm fairly confident that even if kids spend their Pre-K years in beauty school, they'll still somehow manage to eke out a future.

And then there's the cost. You shouldn't have to mortgage your house to get some decent day care for your two-year-old. In fact, many desperate parents have been known to *relocate* just to be closer to the trendiest preschool and will happily fork over twenty grand a year for the opportunity to have their baby learn his ABCs in this special, highly competitive environment—an environment that boasts special tutoring for the early-bird bar exam. If that's your master plan, enjoy your life using food stamps.

When I first started contemplating preschool, it was only because I'd been scared into thinking that if I hadn't chosen one by the first six months of my baby's life, I'd be shut out of any decent school—and that any school with no waiting list would probably also have no teachers or windows. Everywhere I went, it seemed someone wanted to engage me in a conversation about which preschools I had my daughter on the list for. If I made the mistake of telling them honestly that I hadn't chosen one yet, these other moms would look at me like I just dropped my kid off in the woods to be raised by tree squirrels.

When I finally peeled myself off the couch to do a little research, I found that besides there being many types of preschools, people pay as much money to go to a school that they perceive will put their kid on track for Ivy League as they will for a school that's just as happy to let a kid play in a pile of dirt all day if that's where "their delight leads them." I'm no preschool consultant (and yes, they exist), but there seem to be two major categories of preschools: academic and developmental. However, the choice between the two can be polarizing.

A woman I know almost came to blows with her very best friend since second grade over which school would be best for their two-year-olds. My friend, a free-spirited liberal, wanted her daughter in a nurturing environment and was shocked by her previously punk rock, tatted-up, rebellious partner-in-crime's new staunchly academic attitude. It seems Punk Rock had decided that her number one objective for the perfect preschool was that there be school desks. *Desks?* My friend didn't get it. Yes, Punk Rock wanted her daughter to learn to sit at a desk all day and pay attention. She didn't find the preschool where they let kids "just play" all day appropriate. My friend didn't find her friend's *attitude* appropriate. In fact, she strongly suspected that she may have started voting Republican. That was three years ago, and they have yet to make up.

I myself rejected a couple of academic schools right off the bat. The first one didn't want the kids to talk about TV or movies, wear cartoons or logos on their clothes (they actually insisted on a plain, collared polo shirt), or bring sweetened snacks—and I wanted my child to attend a preschool on *planet Earth*, so clearly we had different agendas. Another school quizzed me on where my two-year-old daughter's skills were at in terms of sequencing; summarizing; inferring; knowing her colors, letters, and numbers; and being able to set a table and tie her shoes. Okay, hold on there, genius, I still don't know half that shit.

In my opinion, developmental schools are the way to go, but you have to be careful; under the developmental category you will find some schools that identify themselves as "progressive."

At first the label "progressive" seemed like a plus to me, seeing as I had always been under the impression that progressive meant enlightened, open-minded, and tolerant—yeah, well, not so much. "Progressive" in the context of describing a preschool is just a nicer name for crazy. If a school calls itself progressive, just know that there will be a lot of "children aren't allowed to look into mirrors" or "we only play with plain wooden toys" or "we believe wheat-based food items are the work of Satan" going on. Oh, and you'll pay dearly for the *privilege* of having to send your child to a school with only organic raw veggies to eat in his plain brown lunch sack or face the wrath of the parents' board.

Besides a waiting list, most progressive schools also boast some kind of bizarre philosophy. The first and last progressive school I visited followed what they called "The Democratic Way of Life." In this school you *could* play with a plastic toy, but you couldn't say no—ever. Everything needed to be put into a positive in order to not compromise the child's delicate self-esteem. It was explained to me by a woman with the personality of bait that "We don't say 'sit down.' Sit down is a 'parental agenda,' and parental agendas are not very democratic." Hmm . . . so what do you do when you need your kid to sit their ass in a chair? According to the Democratic Way of Life, you would need to say, "Chairs are for sitting." And then let your child make their own judgment as to whether or not sitting is an activity in which they'd care to participate. *Okay.*

This technique not only sounded fantastic but like something I wanted to immediately incorporate into my life, so when they asked if I'd like to put down a two-thousand-dollar deposit to get my daughter on a waiting list for a possible opening in 2010, I wasted no time in trying it out. Instead of saying, "Hell, no!" I said "Fingers are not for writing checks, fingers are for flipping the bird!"

At that point, I realized it would be in my best interest to eschew the competitive route and look at a couple of preschools with decent reputations but with a more normal price tag. Having heard a rumor about great yet affordable schooling, my next stop was the local neighborhood co-op.

If having kids and a job, cooking dinner, maintaining a house free from flesh-eating bacteria, and squeezing in a shower once a month has left you with way too much time on your hands, then a co-op preschool is just the thing for you. Besides a regular job at the preschool, you will also be invited to enter the exciting world of toilet cleaning, pita pizza preparation, or dead goldfish disposal. Despite the good price, with my busy schedule of reality-TV watching I had a feeling the co-op probably wasn't a good match for my lifestyle.

Finally, after asking around my neighborhood, I found a practically undiscovered gem of a school in the developmental category that had the major advantage of being practically walking distance from my house. Since I'd been scared into thinking there would be a waiting list for any school worth its salt, I headed down to my chosen school a full year early, and despite the fact that they weren't even taking applications for my daughter's class, I forced them to let me put a deposit down so when they *did* start taking applicants I'd already be in there. There, that was done.

But it turns out I still wasn't exempt from the preschool hysteria. The mentality to get kids into the best school is as contagious as a cold sore. First I started feeling a teensy bit disappointed that it had been so easy. Then I got a little suspicious. Had it been *too* easy? Why did they just *let me in?* Why wasn't there a waiting list to get on while my daughter was still in utero? What was wrong with it? Were the teachers all parolees? Was the warm and inviting little classroom secretly a cover for a crack den? Having worked myself into a blind panic, I went back and visited four or five more times, armed with a few questions for the teachers that I'd designed to suss out their weaknesses: "My child doesn't want to eat anything for lunch. What would you do?" "My child is having a rough day and can't seem to get along with anyone. How would that be handled?" "What if my daughter can't stop crying when I drop her off?" "What if *I* can't stop crying?" But these people had an answer for everything! It was *almost* as if they'd heard questions like this before. I found it enormously calming. Plus, I had to be honest with myself, I wasn't willing to make it my life's work to get into one of those elitist schools anyway. I didn't have any friends or family in high places, and I wouldn't have the money to be bribing any schools with a brand-new kitchen or library anytime this decade. Plus, exclusive preschools bring with them exclusive attitudes.

My friend Dinah, who, despite her modest means, spends more on Pre-K than Larry King spends on alimony, told me that although her son is thriving, she's miserable. "At the last fund-raiser, I sat in a corner nibbling organic animal crackers while the super-rich parents discussed whether or not the Amex Centurion card was actually better than the platinum card or just all hype. I just don't fit in." I silently praised God that the moms at my school barely knew one another's names.

This attitude extends to the public vs. private school debate as well. Once at a party a woman briefly engaged me in conversation by asking which private school I had in mind for when my daughter and I were done with preschool. When I innocently replied that I'd heard that the public school in our district was supposed to be really great, my new acquaintance acted like she'd just smelled a sewage leak and took off to commiserate with a woman in a pair of Joe's jeans.

Somehow, school taps into something primal in parents, making them feel they're somehow failing their child by not buying into the hype. We must fight against this nonsense. If you're absolutely set on wanting your child "unschooled" by a Jedi Knight who believes in four hours of homework and only lets the children play with toys made out of fresh-pressed flaxseed oil, then hey, don't let sanity stand in your way. But if you've come to the conclusion that it's *preschool*, then you're way ahead of the game. Of course, that's easy for me to say, because news of my school's greatness has totally caught on and it now has a waiting list mile long!

No matter what the price tag, you should have expectations of a decent preschool. Just be realistic.

REASONABLE EXPECTATIONS

Teachers whom you like and respect.

A monthly cost that doesn't force you to sell your car and switch to public transportation.

Small classes.

No recent cases of the bubonic plague.

A sick kid policy that is strictly adhered to.

UNREASONABLE EXPECTATIONS

A guaranteed spot in the Ivy League college of your choice.

Built-in best friendships with other moms.

Choice of endive or watercress lettuce for your child's catered lunch.

Magazine-quality class photos.

All day, personal, one-on-one attention for your "clearly gifted" child.

Part Three: Who Are You?

A Little Help, Please?

I have a friend, Kim, who told me that when she had her first son, for weeks on end a parade of helpful moms stopped by her house every day with food, gifts, and much-needed assistance. She'd met a large group of women in her hospital birthing class, and once news of her son's delivery hit the mommy network, these moms and moms-to-be quickly organized and sprang into action. Each day, without fail, Kim and her husband received casseroles, lemon-herb rotisserie chicken, apple butter, banana bread, used breast pumps, and nipple cream. These weeks went a long way to softening Kim's transition to motherhood.

When I heard this story, at first I thought she'd just been delirious—possibly from doubling up on her post C-section Percocets—and had fantasized the whole thing, or at the very least maybe she was just retelling a quaint tale she'd read in some 1950s novel about knitting circles. But no, this was true and current-day! Now Kim's about to pop out her second son, and the same women are probably running out right this minute to buy her trashy tabloids or lovingly preparing her a few pints of homemade parmesan cheese dip! I'm so happy for her I could punch someone.

Where was *my* cavalry when I got home from the hospital? Why don't *I* have friends like these? Why wasn't *I* ever asked to my senior prom? God, it's so unfair—or is it? If I'm honest, it's probably my own fault. Having a mess of friends like Kim's in your life requires a lot of maintenance. You need to be the type of person who at the very least remembers birthdays. It wouldn't surprise me if Kim got expensive baby gifts from people she's known since Girl Scouts. I, however shamefully, have trouble keeping my own siblings on my radar, let alone someone I went to summer camp with twenty-seven years ago.

If, like me, you don't have a group of friends who are ready to rally for you after you give birth and well beyond, I'm not going to lie, you will have it tougher. But time is the great equalizer. Eventually, even if you have a slew of great friends, dedicated parents and in-laws, and acquaintances from grade school willing to come lend a hand, people burn out, get busy, or lose enthusiasm, and before you know it, you are left with your infinitely less manageable life.

This is when you must hire help.

Trying to do everything by yourself is simply not possible. Something's got to give, and I promise you, your sanity will just be the tip of the iceberg. And please don't think you'll be fine depending only on your husband or partner, unless you're okay having time for yourself only every other leap year when he agrees to take the kids to the zoo and then brings them back an hour later. Otherwise, get out your wallet. Babysitters, nannies, cleaning help . . . now that you're a parent to one or more children, *you need assistance*. Why is there so much stress and self-judgment around saying, "A little help, please"?

Too much help and you may feel you aren't raising your kid; too little and you can devolve into a grouchy martyr with a house that is incubating the hantavirus. I say, screw the self-criticism! Get as much help as you can. And don't make the mistake of convincing yourself you can't afford it because really, you can't afford *not* to have it.

My friend Crafty Susan, a world-class mom despite her unnatural obsession with decoupage, often struck me as being about one toddler temper tantrum away from downing a bottle of Seconal. It was understandable, since she was raising two boys—one toddler and one infant—with minimal help from a husband who left for the gym every morning at five a.m. and didn't return from his job until ten or eleven every night. I'm not quite sure what he did for a living, but apparently it required rock-hard abs. One afternoon I swung by her house for a playdate and found her sitting on her couch, despondent and teary-eyed.

"I just can't keep up with the clutter anymore. I tried

to clean this pigsty up today, but between breast-feeding, potty training, and sleep deprivation, it's beyond impossible to even wipe off a fucking countertop." Crafty Susan swearing meant things had gotten very, *very* serious. I glanced around her spotless living room, trying to find evidence of mass disorder, but the most offensive thing I could see was a lone DVD out of the case. Her "pigsty" made my living conditions look like the aftermath of Hurricane Katrina; then again, I also didn't make my cake frosting from scratch, so my tolerance for imperfection was a bit higher. But this wasn't about me.

"Why don't you give yourself a break and hire a sitter a couple of hours a week?" I'd made this suggestion many times before.

"I wish I could, but things are tight as it is. We just ordered brand-new living room furniture. There's nothing left over this month." I couldn't help but think, *Do you really need the Shabby Chic chaise, or could that money be better spent giving you two mornings to clear the demons out of your head?* The answer seemed obvious to me. Make it happen.

If the money issue is honestly standing in your way of hiring help—and by that I don't mean by getting help you'd only be able to eat sushi out *twice* a week, I mean that by hiring someone to watch your seven-month-old for two hours you would be giving up baby formula for the next two days—then you will need to get creative.

You do have options; you could arrange sitter swaps, where you hook up with a neighbor or friend and take turns watching each other's kids for an afternoon. If you need babysitting but you're not into watching someone else's kids in return, consider a service swap: This is where someone watches your kid and in return you provide them with another type of service, such as a haircut, something from your homemade handbag collection, or offering to not report them to their condo board for their illegal pet ownership.

If you check around, some churches provide a free or very low cost "moms' day off"; once a week you can drop your kids off for a morning, and in exchange they try to convert you to Catholicism. Not the religious type, but belong to a local health club? Try utilizing your gym's child-care services—but instead of hitting the treadmill, go grab a cup of coffee next door, read a novel, and relax for ninety child-free minutes; just make sure to splash some water on your face to at least give the appearance of being hot and sweaty before you go back to pick up your kid, or you may lose your privileges. Trust me, they tend to be finicky about shit like that. Don't forget about the child labor resources in your neighborhood: For about six bucks an hour you can probably find a twelve-year-old who would be happy to help you out a couple of hours a week. Warning: This doesn't work in L.A. or New York, where most twelve-year-olds refuse to work for cheap because they're saving up for nose or boob jobs.

Finding free cleaning may prove to be a tad more

difficult. Try putting up an ad for a house-cleaning intern on a local college bulletin board; you'll give them the opportunity to help clean up your living environment in exchange for a valuable learning opportunity on the intricacies of dusting and possible college credit. I only recently broke down and hired someone to clean my house once every two weeks, because I thought cleaning help was an extravagance reserved for people too lazy to pick up a sponge—turns out that's me. All I can say is, what took me so long? Lazy or not, it's nice to have a clean bathtub.

Having children changes your circumstances. Even the most self-reliant of us become more vulnerable: Even if you *have* hired help, good friends, and an in-law or two, there will be many times when none of your peeps is available and you will find yourself in a situation where you must break down and ask someone for help outside of your comfort zone. I know it's hard, but don't fool yourself into thinking you can go it alone. You can't.

In fact, this is exactly how I became friends with Kim. I'd spent time with her only on a couple of occasions, but she happened to call me one day when I was deathly ill, had no babysitter, and my husband and most of my friends were at work. Normally, I would've told her I was fine, but she caught me at a vulnerable moment, and I cried to her in desperation on the phone. Kim went from casual acquaintance to comrade in two words: "Come over." I wasn't too proud to argue. Still in the clothes I woke up in, I loaded my daughter in the car with the few toys I could muster up and headed on over. Despite having a toddler of her own and a writing assignment due, she took control. She sent our kids off to play in the backyard sprinklers and settled me on the couch for a few hours of Jerry Springer, herbal tea, and stolen Pudding Pops from the kid's stash. She saved my life that day, and I hope she knows I'd return the favor in a heartbeat.

I fully believe that mothers, with all we give, deserve a guilt-free break as often as possible, whether it's help cleaning, someone to watch our children, or at the very least a therapist to hear about our problems once a week. There's no shame in it—rap stars never go anywhere without a posse to do everything from wipe down their tour bus to refill their drinks, and most rap stars aren't even parents—at least not with custody rights. So whatever your financial situation, do yourself a favor and get yourself some help. Hell, I love my child to death, but I'd gladly sell a vital organ for an afternoon of quiet time. So hey, if anyone wants to buy a slightly damaged liver . . .

The Best-Laid Plans of SAHMs and WAHMs

Although I hate the cutesy, categorizing acronym S-A-H-M, I am a reluctant stay-at-home mom. So sue me. In the never-ending battle of other women telling us the correct way to parent our children, no topic outside of the one involving breast milk sparks quite as much heat as the debate over returning to work as soon as possible vs. sacrificing the career to stay home with your spawn. It's enough to paralyze even the most forward-thinking mother with a morbid fear of doing the wrong thing.

Of course, for millions of moms, there straight-out isn't the luxury of a decision. They have to work—period.

For those fortunate enough to have options, there is no shortage of parenting experts, psychologists, and gender warriors just waiting to dazzle Oprah with their emphatic all-purpose answers on how everyone else should deal with this personal and often agonizing decision. In the current climate of damned if you do and damned if you don't, it's no wonder so many women are filled with doubt and anxiety over their decision.

Most women have some preconceived notion of what they will do postbaby, and I was no different. But what I'm doing now came by trial and error and certainly wasn't at all what I'd envisioned for myself and my life.

I was raised by a full-time working mother. That was all I knew, and I never spent a whole lot of quality time analyzing it. It seemed obvious to me that when and *if* I had a child, it wouldn't need to slow me down a bit. I figured I'd pop the kid out and be back to my career and my old self within a few months. I know I'm not the only one whose hypothetical Babyland was limited to a kick-ass baby shower, being called Mama, and buying cute onesies. It certainly didn't include nuisances like a *real live baby!*

When I was actually pregnant with a nonhypothetical baby and found myself working in television, a field that tends to average a ten-hour day, I started feeling a little less sure of that game plan. Plus my husband, raised by a stay-at-home mom, felt strongly that regardless of the sacrifice, one of us should be home for at least the first year. So given my long hours and the fact that even I knew I'd be too bloated and sleep deprived to work for at least a few months no matter what, I decided, what the hell, I'd give being an SAHM a try.

I even started to look forward to it. A whole year not working! I imagined a full 365 days lying around breastfeeding and watching reality TV—no crazy bosses, no having to "announce" a trip to the bathroom, no traffic, no hour-long commutes, and best of all, no work! I wondered what I'd been resisting. This was going to be fabulous!

But once the baby was here and the initial couple of months of bleary-eyed bonding were over, I soon realized how insanely bored and anxious I was stranded in the house with a companion whose number-one hobby seemed to be spitting up. I started to look to that one-year mark as a beacon of light in an otherwise black hole of laundry, diapers, and bottles. Okay, I'm not including quick runs to the store to pick up another bottle brush and pair of nipple Soothies. Or the lonely walks around the park interrupted only by brief chats with other moms I'd bond with because we had the same Graco stroller and unbond with when I realized that making conversation with a shoe box would've been more stimulating. Life as I'd known it had come to a screeching halt, and I found myself desperately pining for the validation and human contact that came with work.

For a while I made the best of it, hanging out with the few mom friends I'd managed not to scare off, spending time in parks, malls, or wherever corn dogs were sold, and dedicating the remaining time to practicing Kegels, hoping to regain my still compromised bladder control. It was starting to seem like my baby was going to be a nonwalking, nontalking baby *forever*, and I just didn't see how people made this lifestyle work for them. My already shaky resolve was about to be tested.

Against my better judgment, I let my equally bored

but considerably more motivated friend Lara talk me into a free "introductory" music class called Baby's Got the Beat. Sure, it couldn't have sounded less up my alley, but it was free and I had nothing but time.

The group met in a decidedly uninviting, dimly lit room more suitable for an AA meeting than a baby class. The entire place reeked of dirty socks, but again, it was free. So Lara and I sat down in a circle of other moms with their kids. A woman in her sixties who hadn't evolved or detoxed since the Summer of Love floated in and introduced herself as Barbara, "but you can call me Essence." I could see we were off to a bad start. Essence had a whoosh of silver hair, colorful scarves, feather earrings, and most annoyingly, dozens of little bells attached to yellow rain boots. I probably don't need to tell you that it wasn't raining outside.

My daughter immediately erupted in tears from all the jangling. The rest of the babies followed suit, except one kid who was too busy coughing up a lung to cry. Unless he was in the final stages of tuberculosis and his dying wish was to attend Baby's Got the Beat, I wasn't crazy about this kid sitting within drooling distance of my daughter. But there was no way I'd be the paranoid psycho mom who would bring it up.

"Is your kid sick?" I blurted out a whole two seconds later. TB Mom looked at me like I'd just accused her of organizing a terrorist plot.

"It's just allergies," she said with more than a little

hostility in her voice. Yeah, and Lindsay Lohan's problem is just exhaustion. I looked around the room. No one else seemed overly concerned. It figured. They'd probably all downed a couple of boxes of Airborne before heading out. They were *good* moms—moms who knew how to do this. Luckily, TB Mom, who'd apparently been silently seething over my false accusation, suddenly packed up her hacking child's germy belongings and stormed out, giving me a dirty look right as she slammed the door. I felt guilty for all of eight seconds.

And with the threat of consumption cleared, Essence launched into a dissertation of children and music so boring I found it necessary to rewatch an old episode of *Sex and the City* in my head. Jesus, this was going to be a long hour. The class went from bad to unbearable when we finally got to the music portion. The parents were asked to do an interpretive dance around the room while the children beat out a rhythm on drums and triangles. I had just entered my own personal version of hell.

I think it was at precisely that moment I came to the conclusion that if staying home with my daughter meant doing crap like this, it was probably not the best plan of action for my personality type. So, after explaining that my debilitating sciatic hip sadly precluded me from any type of interpretive dancing, I sat frozen through the rest of the class, plotting my escape back to the working world.

At this point my daughter was closing in on a year old anyway, so I decided that looking for work was a reasonable decision. I started letting myself get a tiny bit psyched. I'd have coworkers to gossip about again! Someone else would change diapers and sing "The Wheels on the Bus" forty times to my daughter every day, giving me a chance to miss her. Plus, I figured it would be sweet to be able to afford napkins *and* paper towels again. Color me extravagant, but I wanted both! And since I didn't actually *have* a job yet, I'd have plenty of time to find the perfect situation for my daughter.

Lara had been mulling over her own return to work, so the two of us set about touring local day cares intent on finding a fun, imaginative, loving, nurturing environment for our children—a place much like home, but minus all the expired milk and fuzzy vegetables.

Although they were highly recommended, the first places we saw seemed to have the same scent of dirty diapers and an institutional feel: high chairs and cribs lined up military-style, crying babies, and a ratio of eighty kids to one worker. Okay, maybe it was more like six kids to every worker, but growing panic was not helping me think straight. By the fourth day-care visit, I'd lowered my expectations to "humane" and "fenced in" and Lara, apparently fainter of heart than I'd first perceived, had suddenly stopped returning phone calls.

I continued to make the rounds, determined to find somewhere I could feel semicomfortable abandoning my child. But I wondered how I might leave my precious baby at any of these places. What was I doing? I didn't even have a job! On the other hand, women I respected left their kids here every day, women whose opinions I trusted. Plus, my daughter didn't seem to have any of the same reservations I had; quite the opposite. She was pleased as punch to find toys she'd never had the opportunity to choke on before and a seemingly never-ending supply of juice boxes—which to her utter joy weren't even 100 percent juice! Maybe it was me. Maybe I was losing sight of objective reality.

Over the next couple of months I halfheartedly surveyed and ruled out another few places based on solid reasons like "name of caregiver too hard to pronounce," "no cinnamon oatmeal," and "bad cell phone reception." I might have given up at that point and committed myself to staying home, but right about that time I landed a job interview and (possibly due to my overenthusiasm at just being out of the house) a subsequent job offer.

Here was my chance. I'd done the math and knew a nanny was completely out of the question. After taxes and paying a nanny, what would be left of my paycheck would barely come out to minimum wage. Out of desperation I called a Russian home day care, which I'd heard was "decent" from the sister-in-law of a friend of a woman I had talked to at the library for three minutes. I know. How could it not work out?

I went inside the front door, daughter in tow, and apparently made a wrong turn into the woman's kitchen, where I encountered at least twelve male members of her extended family lounging around in bathrobes, drinking weird-smelling tea, and possibly smoking a hookah pipe. Upon seeing me, they startled like roaches in a New York apartment when you switch the light on too fast. Yeah, I realize a less desperate person would have gone home then and there, but instead, against my better judgment, I allowed the woman to take me on a cursory tour of the backyard.

So I suppose it's my own fault that my daughter got kicked in the face by a four-year-old while I discussed with the owner whether the weekly day care price included borscht. I witnessed the violent assault out of the corner of my eye. The little shit just walked over and clocked my innocent child in the head as hard as he could, then tried to look all nonchalant while my daughter sobbed. I swear he may have hooked his thumbs through his belt loops and started whistling. I momentarily considered kicking the kid back, but I was scared he might be mob connected, so instead I wrapped my baby up in my arms, took her home, and tearfully called to turn down the job, resigning myself to a life of multitasking paper products. What the hell, it would only be another seventeen months and nine days until she'd start preschool anyway.

My sage advice to anyone about to embark on maternity leave is: Don't burn any bridges. You may think you're done with the working world forever, but yelling, "See you bunch of losers on the first of never!" is not attractive for an eight-months-pregnant woman. Worse, it will likely diminish your chances of a smooth return if you should find that being a human diaper-changing machine isn't your life's calling. On the other hand, leaving your personal pictures, snack stash, and *Cathy* mug on your desk because you're 100 percent certain you'll be back as soon as the epidural buzz wears off is a plan sure to backfire once you discover that every second away from your baby is more torturous than a Rob Schneider movie.

It pays to keep your options open.

Back in my role of reluctant stay-at-home mom, I realized that although many women go back to work because they want to, many women don't ever have the choice of not returning to work in an official capacity. I was *lucky*, and it was high time to quit my bitching. Or at least take it down a notch. . . .

All in all, being at home is not so bad; actually, it's pretty cool. It's a relief not having to sneak when I check my e-mail or spend a few hours shopping online. And I don't have to "pretend to work" by carrying around empty files from room to room or quickly switch to a business voice on the phone with my best friend when my boss walks in. Plus, I found that if you get the super-absorbent kind, napkins are every bit as good as paper towels anyway. Of course, just when I'm feeling at peace with my choice, I'll run into a friend whose two-year-old is having the time of her life in day care, and due to her superior socialization, her verbal skills make my daughter look like a shut-in in comparison . . . and I'm right back to square one.

Keeping Up Appearances

We all know motherhood changes a woman in some profound ways. But one of the most visible and disturbing of them is our appearance. Some of these changes are permanent; more cellulite, wrinkles, and bigger feet come to mind. And some are due to lack of time and sleep: bags so heavy under your eyes you need a bellhop, headband overuse to avoid blow-drying hair, and severe razor under-use. So far I haven't found a way around it, and I'm tempted just to accept it, but before we go any further, let's be brave and assess the damages.

Have You Let Yourself Go?

First, take an antianxiety pill and then wait twenty minutes or more, depending on how much you've eaten. Take a look in the mirror under decent lighting. Go ahead. Go. Go! Okay, take another pill. Now give me one. Hurry up. I think we're both ready for this quiz.

1. Look closely (but don't use one of those crazy magnifying mirrors or you'll be immediately put on suicide watch). Do your eyebrows most resemble:
   A) Barbie's
   B) Brooke Shields—the early years
   C) Ben Stiller's

2. Grab your ass—hey, someone has to. Do you feel:
   A) pure steel, baby
   B) kind of like a ball of fresh mozzarella
   C) one of those big sponges you use to wash your car

3. Finish this sentence: The last time I had a manicure was:
   A) earlier this week
   B) earlier this decade
   C) Manicure . . . manicure . . . the word sounds so familiar, and yet . . .

4. Honesty time: Look at yourself naked. Now let your eyes drift south. Would you say your nether region most resembles:
   A) Telly Savalas's scalp
   B) Mr. T's Mohawk
   C) a Macy Gray mess

At this point, I'm assuming you don't have the stomach to continue on with this quiz. Full disclosure: I actually popped one more Xanax between questions three and four. I suggest you lie down for at least half an hour, making sure to avoid looking at your toenails.

I don't know what motherhood does to a woman that makes it almost physically impossible to raise a mascara wand anymore, but from my extensive personal research, I know I'm not alone in this. I truly have little use for makeup, because I only bother to put it on for the rare occasion I leave the house at night without a child. Truth be told, I definitely don't shower as much as the National Health Department would deem fit; many days my teeth aren't brushed until noon; flossing is now a luxury, not a given; I haven't even put on a pair of jeans in I don't know how long; and I've been rockin' the retro bush since I had a child. I've become that woman: The pale-faced, ponytailed, sweats-wearin', worn-out-husband's-T-shirt-sporting, not-a-lick-of-makeup (unless you count my fake bronzing sunscreen) MOM. I used to be kind of cute. I think I still am when I catch a glimpse of myself all done up, but most of the time, I just don't have the energy. No matter how much I loathe that things have gone this way, I feel helpless to turn it around.

There are fleeting thoughts every morning of actually making an effort, and then something happens. A diaper needs immediate changing, the trash needs to go out, the phone starts ringing, I get hungry for waffles and turkey sausage . . . before you know it, it's three o' clock in the afternoon and I still bear a striking resemblance to a slightly more unkempt Bob Marley.

I thought things would be different. I envisioned myself back to my old self once my child got over that pesky infant hump, only with a cute kid/fashion accessory in tow. As it turns out, that was an unrealistic expectation.

"But Stef," you whine at me. "What about women who get up, get dressed, and go to a job every day? They have kids and yet they look great!"

"Ha ha ha!" I laugh in the face of your naïveté. You think that just because a woman has a solid reason to leave the house and mix it up with other adults she has her shit together? Nine times out of ten, I suspect her underwear is on backward, her bra is inside out, and her pants are the same pair she wore yesterday, just with a different top. Oh, and look closely: See that pretty, pale yellow pattern on her shirt? That "pattern" is courtesy of Mott's Apple Juice. Right now she's saying a silent prayer that no one notices it.

If this is your life, and you want to improve it, it's not impossible. But go easy on yourself. Don't bust out of the gate by divorcing your husband and joining a New Age polygamist sex cult in New Mexico where children are not allowed—or even scarier, become a Mary Kay rep. Maybe start by eating at least one meal a day that wasn't handed to you through a drive-through window and then work your way up to wearing pants that don't have an elastic waist. Baby steps. Eventually you can work your way to the gym and go get your roots done. Just think how excited your hairdresser will be to finally see you again! Don't pressure yourself to get back to your old foxy self overnight . . . or ever. Priorities have changed, and that's okay.

I'll admit that there are exceptions to these laws of attraction. Sometimes I'm amazed to see women at the park in their skinny jeans and washed and styled hair, meticulously accessorized kids in tow—looking like models for an Anthropologie ad—and I think, *What's their secret? Do they have a live-in stylist? Is this a photo shoot for* American Baby *magazine? Are they married to David Copperfield?* Luckily, they can't see me staring, because I'm usually wearing smudged sunglasses that take up half my face.

I try to cut myself a break. My reasoning is, parks are like prisons. Why work hard at looking good? If I were in prison surrounded by a bunch of other women, I would spend the bulk of my time eating cashews and working on my science fiction novel, not busting my ass in Pilates and flat-ironing my hair. If you can pull yourself together and go to the park or anyplace else looking like J-Lo without killing yourself, my baseball cap is off to you, but for the majority of moms who can't, please don't waste a moment berating yourself. Most of us are rowing against the tide in the same boat. You'll be back to your old sexy self when your kids go to college. Of course, by then you'll be really, really old . . . okay, *I'll* be really, really old. Damn . . . are Botox places open twenty-four hours?

It's All About Date Night: and Other Urban Legends

Remember when you were in junior high and heard that some kid two towns over was rushed to the ICU after eating Pop Rocks and Pepsi on a dare? A quarter century later the urban legends still abound, only now you're hearing about cool couples whose lives never slowed down postchildren. You know that groovy twosome a friend of a friend met at a party, who take their young kids with them everywhere, make it to dinner, movies, and kiteboarding, and still have the time and energy left for a smokin' sex life? These folktales usually involve free-spirited parents whose children are the ones at the party passed out on the coats at one a.m. while mom and dad pass the bong around like it's still 1989.

Don't believe the hype. You and I both know that life just doesn't work like that. Your social life may not have come to a screeching halt, but it's definitely hobbled, and it's not going to be fully back on its feet for a long time.

Be honest with yourself: When was the last time you and your partner did more together than watch *Grey's*

Anatomy? Sorry, but life has changed. I don't give a rat's ass how many books tell you that you can still look foxy and have lots of sex. After thirteen hours of providing meal service, thinking about cleaning the house, and lying on the floor playing dollhouse with my three-year-old, I usually don't have the energy to run the TiVo myself, much less violate any local sodomy laws. Sorry to be a downer here, but your old life is over!

You, like me, probably used to make fun of those couples who have "date night" once a week. *What a couple of losers,* you thought. *I'll never be that boring and nonspontaneous.* Now you're staring at these couples like they're geniuses who just taught themselves to speak Swahili over a long weekend. *How did they manage to find a babysitter to watch their kids* every *Saturday night? And how can I get a hold of this person and pay them a tiny bit less to watch my kids instead? And most importantly, are they putting out at the end of the night?* Even if they say they are, I have my doubts.

I know for me, a night out with my husband rarely leads to any postdate poking action. Like I said, after a long day, seeing a movie is about all the stimulation I can take for one evening. Plus, I find dinner, drinks, and staying up past nine o'clock to be more sleep inducing than a box of Unisom. I'm not saying that couples with kids don't consummate their dates anymore. Okay, yes, I am saying exactly that.

The suggestion you hear most often in magazines, from therapists and nosy strangers, is to schedule sex.

Nothing will build ardor and desire like sitting down with your husband to plot a time to make hot monkey love on his Google calendar. Be sure to set the "Send e-mail reminder" function if you *really* want to get yourselves worked up. Come on, even if there is a harmonic convergence causing nothing to interrupt your scheduled rendezvous, once you call something an appointment, it feels like obligation, and obligation is not sexy. One or both of you will find that you can't force yourself to be in the right frame of mind.

Another mood killer is bickering, and couples with children have been known to use bickering as their primary means of communication. It doesn't mean there's anything wrong with your marriage—there's just so much more juicy stuff to argue about now! Before kids, the primary disagreements I had with my husband concerned takeout Thai vs. Chinese or whether or not Quentin Tarantino is overrated (he is). Our fights were over within minutes. Now a fight about which one of us does more laundry (me) can escalate into one person storming out of the room (him) and lead to dirty looks (me) for the rest of the day. Although petty bickering itself rarely leads to divorce, it usually isn't the express lane to a night filled with massage oils and the Kama Sutra, either.

I'm not saying married people don't have sex. But realistically, it's not as often. The truth is, I just don't feel quite as sexy as the mother of a toddler as I did when I was simply trying to create one. These days you can find me out of my panties slightly less often than you can find Britney Spears actually *in* hers.

So what's an occasionally horny mom to do? What I find works best for me is to tune into when I am in the mood and not let those opportunities pass me by. If I get the urge and it's the afternoon, I attempt to preserve the feeling and then try getting my husband into the same state of mind as early as possible. And he does the same thing. In this way, we manage to have sex up to once a month! But who's counting?

If you're committed to upping your number of sexual encounters, you'll need to be creative. Pre-kids, sex could be had anywhere, at any time, but now your rendezvous may be limited to rooms with locks on the door. That leaves the bedroom and the bathroom, and who's having sex in the bathroom on a moldy bathmat? If you are, it's time to learn the difference between adventurous and unsanitary. Luckily, most parents always have a crate of Purell on hand. Here's another suggestion: Try adding a lock to your office door. A lot of desk chairs are practically made for close encounters: they're comfortable, sturdy, and often have the added benefit of state-of-the-art back support! And let's not forget the car—tinted windows allow for that extra privacy you need, especially if you only have street parking. And you know all those swivel captain's chairs standard in minivans weren't put there just to make it easier to hand out juice boxes. Just keep a sharp eye out if you're part of the Neighborhood

Watch program: You don't want to miss a crime because you were too busy doin' it in the driveway.

Even if, in spite of your best efforts, your sex life isn't what it used to be, don't feel bad. Despite having the babies out of diapers, having children does change your marriage permanently in some ways. But the good news is that it's probably better in some big ways—much better. Here's where I get a little mushy. Your history as a couple can help you reach deeper understandings, learn to resolve things more constructively, and live through the sex droughts without having a divorce attorney on speed-dial. That said, if you already have a divorce attorney, perhaps you need an altogether different book. You are parents together, and although you share less time, more stress, and more responsibility, you also share the fruits of that responsibility.

Maybe you just need to alter your view of romance. Sure, your last "dinner date" may have been piling the whole family in the car and eating hot dogs at Costco after loading up the trunk. Certainly not as dreamy as that little Italian place where you used to grope each other under the table, but possibly even more fulfilling. Okay, probably not—but you must learn to savor the small moments. Try to make the most of the short time between when you put the kids to bed and when you lose consciousness on the couch: Let the dishes wait until morning (the ants will thank you) and go crazy! Think what you can do in an hour. Watch half a movie!

Drink five glasses of Cabernet! Reminisce about your sex life! Accuse your husband of thinking your best friend has nice boobs! The possibilities for fun are endless, *if* you put in the effort.

But no matter what, parents have a special bond. Every day you have an opportunity to see your children changing and growing, and I don't care how many times I've heard the advice, "Don't spend your only time with each other talking about your kids," some of the greatest moments with my husband have been lying in bed cracking up together over the insanely cute things our daughter did that day. Five years ago I would have been lunging for the insulin, but there you go.

If you find yourself giving in to the drudgery of domestic life and going way too long without sex, here's a little homework to get you back on track: Get a pen and make a list of all the reasons you love your partner. It may just help you find a new appreciation for the guy who not only changes diapers but hangs pictures on the wall, reminds you to get the car serviced, and lends you his T-shirts. Here is my list to help inspire you:

1. He brews a mean cup of coffee every morning.

2. For weeks after Mel Gibson's belligerent, crazy DUI story broke, he referred to me solely as "Sugar Tits."

3. His endless patience.

4. The last time the movie *Another Woman's Husband* starring Gail O'Grady and Lisa Rinna re-aired on Lifetime, he said, "Oh, we've seen this one." And he's not even gay. That I know about.

5. The worst haircut I ever gave myself was introduced to him on our sixth date. He didn't mention it until our sixth year.

6. He doesn't get why men think Pamela Anderson is hot.

7. He knows which episodes of *Dora* are our daughter's favorites.

8. He ends every fight by asking, "Do you want to punch me?"

9. He's the only man I've ever dated who hasn't forced me to sit through *Caddyshack*.

10. He never eats the last popsicle.

After all, it's your partner who gave you the little person or people that make your life so incredibly amazing. It's enough to make you want to run out and buy your husband a Hallmark Special Moments card. But don't. Trust me, it won't lead to sex.

The Newest Addition to Your Family: Stress

There's no doubt about it: Having kids adds to your life. There's more love and more fun, but I'd say the biggest addition to your life after children is stress. If you are one of those people who thought life was incredibly stressful before children—a person who can't tolerate when life is unpredictable, a person who wants to commit hara-kiri when *Lost* is preempted by a presidential speech— you are in for a kick in the crotch when your kid enters toddlerhood. Naptime is no longer a given; leaving the house is no longer a given, considering how often kids come down with colds; mealtime is no longer a given, since one day your kid loves chicken nuggets more than you love a full body massage yet the next day will look at the same meal as if you just threw up on their plate.

It is widely accepted that having a child permanently changes a woman. Studies at Duke University Medical Center show it's not just psychological. There is a stress-related hormone in a woman's body called cortisol that elevates on the birth of the first child and doesn't drop until long after the kids have grown up and been accepted to law school. Yet a lot of women go into this motherhood thing expecting it to completely fulfill their lives. A few years in, I'm sure we all have the sickening realization that, "Damn, as amazing as being a mom is, it's also kind of tough—twenty-four/seven and it's showing no sign of slowing down." Don't let anyone make you feel guilty for acknowledging this fact of childbearing.

Maybe prenatal vitamins should come with a warning label like other prescription medications. You know, the drugs that are meant to make you feel great but have a list of possible adverse reactions a mile long? The commercial for prenatals could show an extraordinarily loving family blissfully frolicking on the beach, while a soothing voice-over quickly rattles off the side effects, hoping you won't notice, "Having children may result in insomnia, hypersensitivity, fatigue, constant complaining, gingivitis, difficulty concentrating, irritability, premature graying, disinterest in sex, a filthy living room, uncontrollable urges to binge on salt-and-vinegar potato chips, mysterious weight gain, a tendency to forget your own phone number, an unhealthy obsession with germs, increased chance of financial ruin, confusion, and psychosis. Consult a doctor before you have children if you're edgy, interested in maintaining a career, or generally sane." Hey, at least we'd know what we're getting into, right? Life with kids is not a Sunny D commercial. It's taxing.

Sure, knowing what we know now, we'd still go ahead and do it anyway, and I truly believe the benefits of having children outweigh the risks to our mental health, but I still think the kid culture misleads us as well as our ticking biological clocks.

One of the bigger shocks to me was that as fun as the toddler years are, in looking back I have to realize in some ways my three-year-old is a lot more tiring now than she was as an infant. Stick a two-month-old in a swing for two hours and they're as happy as Paula Abdul in an all-night pharmacy, but try taking a three-year-old to the park and getting them to enjoy a swing for more than twenty seconds. Not so easy, is it?

Toddlers have the attention span of a house fly, and they're much more destructive. Remember when your toddler was an infant? You could leave her on a blanket in the living room gumming your keys for a half hour while you argued with the cable company in the kitchen. This is an extremely dangerous endeavor with a toddler. Sure, right now your kid is contentedly kicked back on the couch enjoying a little Nick Jr. and a handful of Goldfish, but don't let that glazed look lull you into a false sense of security. Next thing you know, you'll re-enter the room a half hour later only to find that your beige couch is now red-striped, through the magic of permanent markers. And good luck finding the extra money to replace it—chances are if Resolve doesn't get it out, you'll be stuck with the daily reminder of your child's pen prowess until you're off to a retirement home.

One thing that exacerbates stress is feeling guilty for being stressed. There's no shame in our body's natural reaction to the anxiety, tension, and constant worry that accompany parenting. Of course we get a little snappish sometimes. Okay, downright bitchy. So what? We're not Stepford wives, and we shouldn't expect ourselves to be robots! Let's learn to embrace the chaos, because it's too big to fight.

You've heard this advice a million times before, but allow me to reinforce it: Let the house be messy. I know you're thinking, *But then I'll be too embarrassed to have people over to my home.* You know what I say? Good! Hosting guests is overrated—most especially out-of-towners, who not only outrageously expect *clean* sheets but some kind of entertainment agenda every day. Going to other people's houses is so much better, because you can leave whenever the hell you want. When people come to your house and you want to get rid of them, you have to do all that tedious hinting around and then risk the uncomfortable silence when you're forced to yell, "All right people, it's time to go. You don't have to go home, but you can't stay here! Let's go!" That's not relaxing, and feeling relaxed is the ultimate goal.

Another often overlooked way to combat stress: When your brood is in bed at the end of the night, it's not time to unload the dishwasher, toss in the laundry, or update your Quicken. I realize you'll have to do this stuff at some point or risk your house being overrun with ants, running out of clean underwear, and being forced to file for bankruptcy, but don't do it every night. This needs to be your time—and no one's going to hand it to you. You have to *own* it! Don't be a martyr: Order takeout, don't *wash* your underwear—buy more, change the clocks and put the kids to bed an hour early!

But okay, you've figured out a way to secure a splinter of time for yourself, yet you still feel stressed. All you want is a surefire way to unwind at the end of a long day. Not so easy, is it? You know those great articles in *Parenting*, *Cosmo*, *O* or any magazine aimed at women and our busy, busy, stress-filled lifestyles, lifestyles chock-full of bad habits like eating Ding Dongs and yelling at our children? These articles, oh so helpfully, point out wonderfully inventive ways to relieve stress—like how about taking a moment for a deliciously refreshing glass of ice water with a squeeze of lemon instead of stuffing your face with Ben & Jerry's or slapping your kid?

Come on, ladies! Why are you shouting at your neighbor because his dog just pooped on your lawn for the fourteenth time today when you could be doing some *ohm*-inducing YOGA? Okay, take a deep breath. Allow me to give you some more realistic alternatives to taking a bath with rose petals, since we all know that rose petals are a bitch to clean out of the tub.

1. Get a tattoo! Let loose and go get a tattoo with the names of all of Brad and Angelina's kids on your lower back. Be sure to leave enough room for many new additions.

2. Take ten minutes to imagine a little sexual healing with Anderson Cooper.

3. Sing "Wind Beneath My Wings" at the top of your lungs for the security camera at the entrance of the grocery store. Hope to get discovered.

4. Make more time for Twinkies. A lot more time.

5. Kick your kids' *Happy Feet* penguin down a long staircase as hard as you can while your child isn't looking. Later, when they ask why "Mr. Mumbles" isn't singing anymore, tell them he's sleepy.

6. Three words: Amateur Strip Night.

7. Get some dental work done just for the Percocet, become addicted, and then if

insurance covers it, kick your addiction at Crossroads in Antigua for at least ninety days.

8. Try a cool, refreshing glass of iced vodka with a squeeze of lemon.

Kiddie Couture

Yesterday my three-year-old daughter wore green camouflage pants with a red and black tutu and a tiara—and she totally pulled it off! She reminded me of a tiny Sarah Jessica Parker after raiding the wardrobe closet at *Vogue*. A woman even stopped on the street to take her picture. Trust me: This pint-size hipster flair was completely spontaneous, self-generated, and mostly a fluke. Still, I have to admit I was a little jealous. No one's ever stopped to take a picture of *me* in my banana clip and flip-flops.

When it comes to fashion and music, I'm not what you'd call cutting edge. I don't listen to Bloc Party, all my tattoos are water soluble, and I once had to be physically restrained from buying a Clay Aiken CD. I got my belly button pierced at *thirty*—and then spent more money to have it taken out a week later because it kinda hurt. I started wearing Isaac Mizrahi . . . just as soon as he released his line in Target. Feel sorry for me if you want, but I'm okay with the way I am.

To my credit, I've never used emoticons, but I *could*

because I'm on AOL. Exactly. I still have an AOL account. Even my in-laws have moved on to Gmail but here I am, still looking forward to my morning's "You've Got Mail."

Of course, my kid's cutting-edge clothing style, as with that of most kids, is mostly accidental. Left to her own devices, she'd just as soon cover her body with yellow Post-its and call it an outfit. And if asked to change into something more appropriate, she might reappear with one leg warmer, swim goggles, and a poncho.

Kids are natural dorks. Childhood is the demilitarized zone of self-consciousness—the one point in your life (short of the bliss of senility) when you are utterly free to indulge your whims, unrestrained by the harsh confines of style or fashion. If you don't instruct most of them otherwise, kids will freely match stripes with paisley, proudly wear 100 percent polyester, and see nothing wrong with wearing footie pajamas to the grocery store. Not only do I not care, I love it! I cherish *my* inner dork and wouldn't think of letting my daughter suppress hers.

Even if we once managed to attain a modicom of cool, at some point, with high school safely fading in the rearview window, most of us stop putting such a high premium on this elusive quality. By the time that we're shaping or warping our own offspring's minds, most of us have grown up enough to just let our kids be kids. Most of us. But not all of us. There are still the moms in every group who would sooner die than have their baby sporting a *Sesame Street* character on a T-shirt from Sears and demand only two-hundred-dollar Juicy Couture from Nordstrom.

I mostly don't understand the new genre of hipster parents who proudly refuse to let their kids listen to kids' music or watch kiddie TV, and insist on decking their pocket-size prodigies out in ironic T-shirts and baby Vans. Living in Los Angeles, not a day goes by that I don't spot a "too cool" parent (L.A. and New York being prime habitats). For those unfamiliar with the species, the Too Cools—or Tools, if you will—amplify the average parent's grudging resistance toward the cloying tone of children's culture and turn it into a postpunk rebellion against the utter *uncoolness* of childhood.

In the hands of a Tool, those tedious years between birth and elementary school need not be marred by anything as mawkish as "Guess How Much I Love You?" or as utterly suburban as *Dora the Explorer*. Not when a size 2T "Iggy Pop" T-Shirt and a skull-emblazoned scooter can give even a two-year-old instant street cred.

It makes me cringe. It's like the Too Cools think they were the first to realize that thirty minutes of Elmo's voice can induce homicidal thoughts, or that there's one thirtyish guy (usually on bass) in almost every popular kids' band who gives adults that skeevy feeling. We all know that, and we wish to God our shorties actually preferred the Lemonheads to Laurie Berkner, but they don't—so we man up and endure.

It's our *job* as parents to put up with a certain amount

of this shit. It's in the contract we all signed before we popped them out. If you don't believe me, check the fine print.

The reality of this bargain was vividly driven home recently when I took my daughter to see Go, Diego, Go! Live at the Kodak Theatre in Hollywood, starting with the box office line filled with enough Mom Jeans to make a stretch panel that could snap to the moon and back.

At least I knew I was in the right place. The lobby was pure pandemonium. I waited too long to buy tickets and got shut out of the prime eleven a.m. and four p.m. shows. Stuck with the nap-killing two p.m. matinee, my daughter and I entered a lobby teeming with overtired toddlers amped by countless juice boxes into a menacing pre-Diego frenzy. Event security isn't allowed to use a choke hold on four-year-old boys, but I didn't flinch from hip checking a couple of them who almost knocked the animal crackers out of my daughter's hand as they made a rush for their seats.

Soon the lights dimmed, and a doughy-looking man in khaki shorts swung tentatively onto the stage on a vine. What I momentarily mistook as the ghost of Steve Irwin turned out to be our star. "Diego" looked like he was at least forty-five and hadn't had done a pull-up or crunch since the mid-nineties. I'm not 100 percent sure because I've only watched the TV show about *four million times*, but I don't think preteen animal rescuer Diego is supposed to have a receding hairline! Then, about halfway through,

Dora herself made a guest appearance. Let's just say that the purple shorts weren't doing her very adult J-Lo ass any favors. Don't these actors have to dance at least forty-five minutes a day? I know I sound harsh. Maybe it was the sugar crash from the entire bag of concession-stand Jelly Bellys making me irritable. And okay, maybe I shouldn't have expected Broadway, but it wasn't like they were working a kids' birthday party or a Carnival cruise—this was the national touring company!

But then, of course, I looked down at my daughter, and it was like we were at two different shows. "Dora!" she squealed, as if Bono himself had just taken the stage. She had died and gone to Diego heaven. She jumped around, holding her cardboard Baby Jaguar mask to her face, exuberantly "growling like a jaguar" on Diego's command. In truth, her joy was so contagious that when at last Diego saved Baby Jaguar's growl, even I had to admit it was pretty darn cool. This is what they live for at this age. I challenge any Tool to get this kind of reaction from a three-year-old forced to endure a Rage Against the Machine show.

When it comes to music, in my experience, kids like catchy songs with lyrics they understand, and then they like those songs to be played again and again and again and again . . . until you're forced to "lose" the offending CD when a gust of wind rips it from your hand and straight through the car sunroof (never hesitate to exploit the fact that kids have no concept of aerodynamics). It's true that children can like listening to anything they're exposed to on a regular basis. We're all like that. Eventually, no matter how unlikely it is that we'll find something the least bit tolerable, through overexposure we may begin to enjoy it. How do you think Justin Timberlake got so popular?

That said, be careful what you play for your kids, as it can lead to some disastrous results. In the sixth grade I was invited to a friend's birthday party. Okay, not exactly a friend, more like a popular girl whose mother made her extend an invite to all her sixth-grade classmates. I obsessed on what to get her for a present and decided on a record—not just any record, but my all-time favorite record—because it was my *mother's* favorite record, Janis Ian. Angsty, armpits-unshaved, "At Seventeen"–singing Janis Ian. Even my mother expressed reservations, thinking it might not get the best reception. But in sixth grade, due mostly to overexposure, I *loved* Janis Ian. I cried and sang along in my room, wishing I was a folksy, twentysomething, unruly-haired singer who could make peoples' hearts ache with a specific chord change—and wear a beret without getting heckled.

At the birthday party, I presented my gift with bated breath, waiting to finally be accepted, perhaps even celebrated for my good taste. My heart swelled with pride while she unwrapped it. But the recipient, Brenda Hoffman, gave me a look of pity I'll never forget. I'd gotten it so wrong, and they all knew it. Smirks gave way to laughter and exclamations of "Who the hell is Janis

Ian?" while I sulked in the backround. Debbie went on to open Shaun Cassidy, the Bee Gees, Olivia Newton-John, and other far less navel-gazing lesbians, apparently more appropriate for a ten-year-old girl.

And that story is precisely why I keep my current Tori Amos obsession well hidden. I have let my attempts at coolness go, and it's a relief.

Don't get me wrong, I haven't gone completely to the dark side. I may be currently on the cusp of my first minivan purchase, but until the deal is sealed, I'm clinging to visions of me in a badass black Acura SUV like a preteen ogling electric blue eye shadow. Okay, a preteen in 1981, but you get the point. And in spite of my fear of raising a daughter as unhip as her mother, these things often have a way of working themselves out. Yesterday my daughter told me, "I hate Barney. He's stupid!" Besides her ability to throw an occasional avant-garde ensemble together, along with Gwendolyn and the Good Time Gang, Laurie Berkner, and *The Best of Sesame Street*, she also requests Foo Fighters, Neil Young, and early James Taylor (she prefers something from the heroin years) as her bedtime music. The girl wouldn't know the Wiggles if they bit her in the Pull-Ups. She loves to have her toenails polished and can put on eye shadow (for fun) more attractively than I can. Unfortunately, her current favorite song is that horrible Chumbawamba "I get knocked down, but I get up again" song that it took the latter half of the nineties to clear out of my head. And she dances like you'd expect a three-year-old to dance to Chumbawamba. But hey, if worse comes to worst and she does eventually turn out like her mom, I know I'll always have a friend in my tragic unhipness. And that's pretty damn cool in its own way.

In Praise of Praise

I praise my three-year-old daughter with wild abandon. When my junior Picasso shows me a drawing she just lovingly scribbled in broken crayon, my heart swells with pride, and I don't try to hide it. "How beautiful! I love it!" I'll exclaim. There are many other accomplishments, big and small, that elicit a similar reaction: listening well, doing the things I ask her to do, tasting a new food, saying please and thank you, really loud burps, and informing me when she's pooped her pants all rate high on my list of things to celebrate. Many times I give her props for just being her. I love the way she lights up like a Christmas tree when she sees how pleased I am with her latest accomplishment and how my encouragement seems to make her even hungrier to try new things.

Yes, I'm *that* parent—the *Free to Be . . . You and Me* generation, the Marlo Thomas mom who grew up with Mister Rogers lacing his Keds, buttoning up his cardigan, and letting me know in no uncertain terms that I was special. Sure, he may have looked at me a little *too* intensely, sort of like he just caught me fantasizing about shoplifting and intended to save my soul through puppetry, but his message hit its target: Kids should like themselves.

But recently I found myself in the company of a woman who had a very different parenting style. Having just introduced myself to a seemingly cool new neighbor in her front yard, I couldn't help but give her eleven-month-old son a little squeeze while whispering, "What a cutie" in his ear. Out of nowhere I found myself being reproached.

"Oh no, no, no, no!" she scolded as she scooped her son out of my grasp, planting him firmly back on the lawn. "We only give Caden very specific praise if he's done something well, and we avoid empty compliments and overpraising him."

Whaa? I must've looked at her like she'd just told me her family practiced cannibalism, because she quickly followed with, "We don't want him to turn into a narcissist," as if that would clear it all up for me.

It turns out that she and her husband had hopped on a new parenting bandwagon that claims that the self-esteem movement has turned our children into little egomaniacs. Haven't heard of it? Well, I checked it out, and apparently there were a few studies that received mass media attention, basically claiming that more college students than ever before are scoring above average on an evaluation that tests for narcissism.

The studies pin this trend on overpraising and telling

children they're special. Most notably a study from a Professor Jean Twenge of San Diego State University, who says "We need to stop endlessly repeating, 'You're special' and having children repeat that back. Kids are self-centered enough already." I'm sorry, but doesn't Professor Jean sound like a crabby old biddy? The kind who can easily spend an hour bitching about the price of coffee at Coco's and angrily shushes children in movie theaters? This is who we're going to for parenting advice? She sounds less like a psychologist and more like someone who's been working at the DMV for the past forty years.

I badly wanted to point out the obvious to my new neighbor: Your kid is only eleven months old. What are the chances he would recognize his own face in the mirror at this age, let alone get a swelled head from hearing how cute he is?

New studies come out every day that can scare the good sense out of parents. Naturally, the studies that get the most attention invariably warn parents that the way they have been doing things is completely wrong, but that luckily for us, the "experts" have figured out the right way to do it just in the nick of time, before our children become meth heads, psycho killers, or God forbid, B minus students with no chance of ever holding a job that doesn't involve wearing a hairnet.

I'm not saying these studies are completely without merit, I'm just saying we don't need to go overboard and start ignoring our own instincts based on the latest scare: *Does Day Care Damage Your Child? Is TV Making Kids Fat? Ritalin Use Doubles in Children of Divorce: But the Question Remains, "Why?"* I DON'T KNOW! But I'm going to have to up my Zoloft by about 100 milligrams before I read any more studies. Sometimes ignorance is bliss.

The scarifying onslaught of new information is certainly not limited to parenting, yet somehow we are able to brush it off and not alter our entire lifestyle when we hear that a glass of white wine can shave a year off your life, chocolate contains more mercury than an ocean full of tuna, or dating Colin Farrell may cause herpes. Why can't we be as picky with our parenting? Some nervous parents act as if making their own parenting choices is akin to cutting their own bangs; they don't trust themselves and fear every decision they make is sure to yield irreversible results. But come on, only you know your child. What ever happened to using our natural instincts?

Call me a crazy radical, but new studies be damned; I want my daughter to have self-esteem. When she sings me a song, I tell her that I love her singing—and why the hell not? So what if she's no LeAnn Rimes? Worst-case scenario, she becomes deluded enough to one day audition for *American Idol*. I look on the bright side: With enough false confidence and entitled attitude, she'd probably make the final twelve.

Sometimes my daughter sees a picture of herself (it's hard not to, since they're everywhere in our house) and exclaims, "What a cute little girl." Sure, my confidence-killing neighbor might worry that it means she's vain and enroll her in a self-esteem-lowering workshop without delay, but she's three! Have you ever seen a seventeen-year-old say, "I'm a pretty girl"? No, most teenage girls are too busy worrying that their size two ass is humongous and keeping their food intake down to four carrot sticks a day. The fact is, my daughter, like most three-year-olds, *is* a cute little girl, and I'm not worried she'll still be saying it at seventeen; I'm more concerned that she won't.

What's wrong with a little overpraising? Say what you will about the stereotypical Jewish mother, but these "overpraisers" seem to have a lot of kids in the Ivy League. Walk into any strip club and try to find a Tovah on the pole. You won't—she's too busy studying for the bar exam. Or maybe we Jewesses just aren't good dancers. . . . I prefer to believe the former.

Let's just agree to allow common sense rule over paranoia. The "don't overpraise" advice may be fine, even important, when applied to older kids and teens who are well aware when you're lying. Who can deny that proclaiming every kid on the high school varsity basketball team a "winner" leaves little to strive for? And is specific praise better than general praise? Sure. Which would you rather hear your partner say, "Great dinner, sweetie" or "This pad Thai is perfect! How smart of you to order from our favorite takeout place again!"? Of course specific praise rules the day—it shows that the person admiring you is actually paying attention and not just doling out empty words. If that makes the difference to the next generation, then by all means go to town—but if some all-purpose praise slips out, cut yourself a little slack. Kids aren't scoring the winning touchdown every day, and sometimes you're just not feeling that creative. A light dose of general kudos is not going to turn your child into a future meth mouth or community college dropout, nor will they automatically become a vapid, narcissistic Paris Hilton. Just maybe they will become a well-balanced human being. Now, excuse me while I go tell my daughter she's special.

Going for Broke—or a Second Baby

As I start this chapter, I am five weeks pregnant. So, at forty years old (aka advanced maternal age, aka a fossil), I've been told there's a very good chance I will miscarry. In fact, the doctor who did an extremely early ultrasound at just *under* five weeks, despite my positive pregnancy test, found nothing in my uterus and, oh so gently, told me that the chances of me going on to have a healthy pregnancy were about fifty-fifty.

"It could go either way," as he so delicately put it, shrugging his shoulders for emphasis.

Now, I'm a poker player, and fifty-fifty are not good betting odds. I'm certainly not throwing all my chips in the pile on fifty-fifty, so those statistics are making me incredibly anxious.

But wait, I'm getting ahead of myself. Two months ago I wasn't at all sold on the thought of another baby. Yet now I'm comforting myself with that fact that I'm tearing up over an especially touching episode of *Sponge-Bob* and thinking I may have underestimated Enya's vocal talents. Medically speaking, this tells me my hormones are in overdrive and my pregnancy is moving forward. Also, my regular breasts feel like they've been mysteriously replaced with twin hills of wet, packed cement and the thought of wine makes me queasy, which is, like, wrong.

But this is not a book about pregnancy. You've all been pregnant, and I'm assuming that if you're reading *this* book you've got a mound of pregnancy books growing dust on your shelf. We don't need to hear any more about my belly. So let's get back to my brain.

How did I get here? How did I go from undecided to inconsolable? Good question. Unless for some reason you were lobotomized, you, like me, found the first year of having a baby extremely taxing on every part of your life. But after the first eighteen months or so, the lack of sleep, brain-numbing boredom, and constant anxiety were taken over by one pure thought: What if I'd never had this child? No matter how rough the beginning is, I can't imagine *anyone* is exempt from contemplating having another child after falling so madly in love with their first one. But how does one go from contemplating to going for the gusto?

When deciding whether or not to have another baby, some serene people "just know" the right choice for them. These types of people have probably never tried the "cookie diet" and expected to lose weight, they've never polled a hundred friends before deciding whether to cut bangs, and I'm sure they've never wondered what it would be like to do heroin. I'm not one of those lucky few.

I tortured my poor husband for months with proclamations of "One child is perfect for us! I'm *totally* fine with just having our daughter." After all, I was pretty sure I'd heard it's the second child that destroys your marriage, drains your finances, and forces you kicking and screaming into a Toyota Sienna. So I was happy and settled with my decision, sure that I had single-handedly saved myself from life as a broke, single parent of two.

For about a day and a half. Then I was back to square one.

I'd see parents with two kids and think how perfect they looked. One for each! I'd look at my little girl and feel sad picturing her all grown up and alone in the world, without any siblings to get together with and bitch about their horrible upbringing. Knowing how much I'd come to love this child, I wanted another. I wanted to feel that indescribable, all-encompassing love—times two! One day I spent some time with my friend Lara, who had just brought her second baby home from the hospital. Smelling that new baby boy smell was all it took to send me right over the top, and I came home adamant about going for number two.

My husband felt the same way, but being the more sensible one, when I brought it up for the thirteenth time he said, "I want you to feel this way consistently for at least a week. If at that time you still want to, we'll try." A whole week? I *know*. What a tyrant! I've never even had a favorite color for an entire week.

So I set about trying to figure out if another baby was the right avenue to take. I wrote out the pros and cons.

Pros:
Another baby to love
That new baby smell
Demerol in the hospital

Cons:
Inevitable homelessness
No sleep again ever
Aging another ten years
Being the oldest mom on the planet
Diapers, diapers, diapers, diapers
Privacy a thing of the past
Gaining seventy-five pounds—again
Giving up another room of the house, which we
   don't have
Postpartum depression
Not being able to afford luxuries like groceries
Having to hang out with other moms with infants
Possible colic

My decision was obvious. So seven days later, ovulating and buzzed on two glasses of Pinot Grigio (fine, three glasses of cab), around midnight, I date-raped my husband. By three a.m. I was coming up with baby names. By eight a.m. I was out buying pregnancy tests. What is it about one night of attempting to make a baby that makes a relatively sane woman start buying home pregnancy tests in bulk? Not only that, but somehow it seems perfectly reasonable that you'll see that little pink "you're knocked up" line the *day after you try to conceive.* Come on ladies, settle down. You have to wait at least two days.

So, trying to remain calm, four days before my period (which would indicate my failure to have successfully reproduced), I took the test. After waiting the requisite three minutes, I felt certain that I could make out a faint line. But just to be sure I didn't hallucinate it, I took three more tests. Unfortunately, they yielded the same nebulous results. I knew I needed to either wait a couple of days *or* . . . get more tests.

This is when I had the brilliant idea to purchase five tests from the 99 cents store. I could take tests to my heart's content and be slightly less than five dollars poorer for my neurosis. The great thing about the 99 cents store is it's the only place you can find leg warmers and jalapeños in the same aisle. So as not to seem obsessed with pregnancy tests, I bought a few other things: a scented Jesus candle, a boxer dogs calendar from 2005, and a tube of toothpaste with the suspicious brand name "Cresta."

I brought my purchases home and headed straight for the bathroom.

Quickly I ripped open the first test, peed like a woman on a mission, read the *Details* magazine sitting on the toilet top for twenty seconds, then looked to see the results. But I couldn't figure it out. Yes, even with my high school education and one creative writing class in college, I couldn't discern if it was positive or negative. I grabbed the box for instructions but got no help there.

The directions were insane. There were three pictures of your possible results: one is *pregnant*, one is *not pregnant*, and one is "you didn't do it right, idiot." Guess what? They all looked *exactly the same*. You probably don't believe me, so I am including a visual.

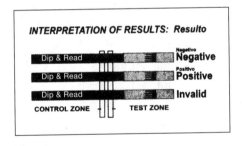

See? What would you do? I decided to call the 1-800 number and get to the bottom of this. Naturally, it's an *international* call. Before it connects you with a live operator, you are informed that if you would like to continue the call it will cost $5.49. Hello! I paid less for the damn tests.

Finally I admitted defeat, waited a few days, and bought myself another real home pregnancy test. Well, I call it a real test; some might call it "Ask Magic 8-Ball." But the news was good and, better than that, easy to read: "Signs point to yes." Sure enough, soon after, I found myself knee-deep in nausea. And that is how I ended up in the office of Dr. Fifty-Fifty for my early visit. Everyone in the Valley goes to this doctor. He's *the best*, I've been told.

While I was checking out of the office, after the disheartening news of my bad odds, I couldn't help but notice, on the wall, large pictures of this doctor posed with B-level actresses and their babies, whom he either delivered or borrowed for a showbiz photo op. I felt myself getting irrationally angry. Hey, it's not a fucking dry cleaner, it's a doctor's office! I don't need to know you delivered Heather Locklear's baby. Wouldn't that be a better spot for your *medical degree?* And then I started wondering if this was an isolated incident. Did other doctors' offices in L.A. do this too? Was there a urologist somewhere in Hollywood with a framed headshot of Danny Bonaduce on the wall? It was all too much. I immediately lost my lunch in the bathroom reserved for urine specimens.

I decided then and there I'd need to switch doctors, and thanks to my habit of doing next to no research, I had an appointment for the following week.

My new doctor was exactly my type, no nonsense,

no unnecessary pessimism, and best of all, no pictures on the wall of Heather, Lisa Rinna, Denise Richards, or any other Lifetime movie staples. My ultrasound showed a healthy seven-week-old baby with a strong heartbeat. And I burst into tears. "Everything looks perfect," said my new favorite person on the planet, and I was sent home with some prenatal vitamin samples to continue puking in earnest.

Everything was going fine until one night a week later when while lying in bed coasting to sleep on a half a Unisom (safe in pregnancy, so don't start with me!), a B-6, and a calming episode of *Snapped* on Oxygen, I felt something unusual. Wet. Scary. Oh shit, blood! When I moved the covers over, it wasn't a few drops but more like a scene out of *Saw*. I didn't want to immediately sink to Dr. Fifty-Fifty's level, but this was not looking good. I screamed for my husband, paged the good doctor, and continued to gush blood while my husband zoomed me to the ER (which we all know is my favorite place). It certainly didn't help calm me down that they rushed me straight into a room with no waiting. Hey, doesn't the guy with the head wound seem worse off than me? No?

I figured a miscarriage was the foregone conclusion, which is what the ER doctor figured as well, so I resigned myself to watching the World Series of Poker with my worried husband while we waited for an ultrasound tech to arrive and confirm the bad news.

About seventeen hands of poker later, I had goo on

my stomach and the technician was about to tell me the fate of my baby. "Your beautiful, healthy baby is still here and . . . doing just fine! Heart is beating one hundred fifty beats a minute . . . that's great . . . oh, and your other baby is doing great too."

"What the fuck did you just say?" were my exact words. Classy, I know.

"Congratulations, you're having twins." And then I looked at my husband, and I think we both passed out from fear, shock, confusion, and lastly, relief.

So now, as I finish this chapter, many ultrasounds later, I may have reached a point of acceptance and can even laugh about it—of course, even the slightest giggle already causes me to leak a little pee. Despite the aches and pains, I am, in fact, looking forward to delivering twin *girls* in just a few months, drinking for three, and contemplating a next book: *Better Make Mine a Double*.